MOST HIGH

reading 1-2 Samuel like God is the main character

Copyright © by Delight Ministries
All Rights Reserved
Book design by Faith Hyman
Theological Editing by Aubrey Johnston
Editing by Maddie Grimes

No part of this book may be reproduced in any form or by any electronic or mechanical means including information storage and retrieval systems, without permission in writing from Delight Ministries.

All Scripture quotations, unless otherwise indicated, are taken from the Holy Bible, New International Version®, NIV®. Copyright ©1973, 1978, 1984, 2011 by Biblica, Inc.™ Used by permission of Zondervan. All rights reserved worldwide. www.zondervan.com The "NIV" and "New International Version" are trademarks registered in the United States Patent and Trademark Office by Biblica, Inc.™

Delight Ministries
www.delightministries.com

Printed in the United States of America
First Printing: January 2025
Color House Graphics
ISBN: 978-0-578-94404-3

Our Mission

Our mission is to invite college women into **Christ-centered community** that **fosters vulnerability** and **transforms stories.**

Christ-Centered Community

We launch, grow, and **sustain thriving Christ-centered communities** on college campuses. We've seen time and time again that community is often the catalyst for **true Kingdom impact.**

Foster Vulnerability

We aim to provide a **space on college campuses** for women to vulnerably share how Christ has been at work in their lives. We believe that vulnerability leads to **breakthrough, and breakthrough leads to transformation!**

Transform Stories

We believe that **one moment with Jesus can truly change everything.** Our mission is to give college women numerous opportunities to meet with Jesus and **have their lives transformed!**

TABLE OF CONTENTS

01
Chapter 1
God Who Hears
/ PAGE 18

02
Chapter 2
Intimate God
/ PAGE 40

03
Chapter 3
Jealous God
/ PAGE 58

04
Chapter 4
God Who Sees
/ PAGE 78

05
Chapter 5
God of Victory
/ PAGE 96

06
Chapter 6
God and Friendship
/ PAGE 114

07
Chapter 7
Holy God
/ PAGE 132

08
Chapter 8
God, Worthy of Worship
/ PAGE 150

09
Chapter 9
God Who Forgives
/ PAGE 166

10
Chapter 10
God Who Delights
/ PAGE 184

How to Read this Book

Scripture

In this study, we'll be walking through the books of 1 and 2 Samuel. These are amazing books of the Bible full of important moments, so we won't be able to cover everything. Instead of a verse-by-verse breakdown of the entire books, you can think of this study as an exploration. We're cruising through the text and pulling out specific moments we feel called to focus on for this study—moments where we see glimpses of the character of our Most High God. If you want to read the parts we weren't able to cover on your own time, we totally recommend it!

Each week you'll be reading anywhere from a few verses to a few chapters of Samuel as we work our way through the book. The chapters in this study will walk you through the reading process. As you read, you'll answer questions, fill in the blanks, and hopefully get a deeper understanding of the context behind what you're reading. You'll want to pull out your Bible and start reading anytime you see something like this . . .

> Read 2 Samuel 22:14.

Just remember that this is your cue to pause and open the Word. Please don't skip reading the actual Word of God! We promise that our words pale in comparison to what God can say to you directly through Scripture! Primarily, we will use the NIV translation when citing Scripture throughout this study. Feel free to use whatever translation works for you, but you might be a tad confused on some of the fill-in-the-blanks if you use a different Bible translation. You can always head to BibleGateway.com to access a free version of the NIV if you need it.

Each week, we will zero in on a topic that the Scripture introduces, using three main points to guide our journey through the text. Our prayer is that this book brings new light to Bible stories and verses that you've perhaps read a million times.

Think it Through

You'll notice that all throughout the book, we ask you questions under the title "Think it Through." These questions are your opportunity to take it deeper, to do some personal reflection and allow the Scripture to begin to soak into your heart and life. These are moments of evaluating where you're at and embracing the hard truth. Don't just answer how you think you should answer; answer as honestly as possible! There is such freedom to be found when we come before the Lord with all of our mess and imperfections! We promise that as you get vulnerable before the Lord, He will unlock even deeper intimacy.

Conversation Starters

Our goal is to get the conversation rolling between you and the Lord, within your Delight community, or through a small group! These questions found at the end of every chapter will help you do just that. We suggest setting some time aside each week to think through your answers to these questions in a prayerful way with the Lord. Then, come ready to discuss them with whoever you're processing this study with. We promise that the more time you take to prepare on the front end, the better your conversations will be!

Take Your Time

Remember that you have an entire week to get through each chapter! Don't feel like you have to do it all in one sitting. Take your time with it and try to process and understand every last verse. There's no pressure to get through an entire chapter in one day. Break up the content however works best for you!

Tips for Reading Scripture

The truth is, reading Scripture isn't always easy! It's a muscle that you have to stretch and grow over time. We've compiled a list of tips from some of our friends that will help you to start to love your daily time in the Word. These are all practical tips that will help you to better hear the voice of God through the Scripture.

#1 Prepare Your Heart: This is SO simple! Every day before you open the Word, ask God to simply prepare your heart, show up, and speak to you. Reading the Bible isn't something we have to do on our own or through our own power. The Word is alive, meaning that God can and will speak to you through it. All you have to do is ask!

#2 Ask Good Questions: This can seriously change the way you encounter the Bible! The best tool we have to understand the Word of God is our ability to ask the right questions. If you've ever read Scripture and not understood something (a.k.a. us every day of our lives), that's an invitation to ask a question. What? When? How? Where? Who? Why? Dig into your questions and seek out answers!

For some of your more historical or practical questions, you can read biblical commentaries, get a study Bible, or talk to someone you trust with more biblical knowledge or Bible study experience. For the other more complex questions, bring them to the feet of Jesus and simply ask. He cares and can provide answers in some of the coolest ways! This isn't your college calculus class where you have to be afraid of looking stupid. There is a loving, caring, and gentle Father on the other end of the line ready to have dialogue with you. *If this is new to you . . . don't worry! We're going to ask A LOT of questions about the text together in this book.

#3 Read at Your Own Pace: Take your time with reading Scripture! You have your entire life to read the Bible. If you want to meditate on one verse for an entire week, do it! If you want to read the entire Bible in a month, do that! Go at the pace that feels comfortable to you. Don't be afraid to slow down and dive really deep in certain parts when you feel led to.

#4 Talk About It: Some of the best moments of revelation from Scripture happen by simply talking about the things you've been reading. This isn't a journey you have to travel alone! Be sure to talk about how God is speaking to you through His Word with your roommate, friends, parents, and your Delight community!

#5 Follow the Spirit: When you're reading your Bible, don't be afraid to change course from where you initially started. You may start out reading Genesis but then feel a nudge to reread that Psalm you heard the other day. Don't ignore those nudges! When you open up your heart to hear from the Lord, He may redirect you to another passage of Scripture. And that is absolutely OK. You never know what He might be leading you to.

Before We Begin

A TikTok video has been playing on repeat in the back of my mind the whole time I've been writing this study. I was scrolling through my feed when a sermon snippet from a pastor wearing cool loafers and a beanie popped up. Usually I skip through those types of videos because I prefer when my algorithm delivers dog videos, but I stopped and watched this one because he used the word "hermeneutical," which I thought was fancy (just keeping it real, ladies).

Anyway, this pastor was talking about his approach when it comes to interpreting Scripture (that's what *hermeneutics* means, in case you felt the need to Google it like I did). To explain the way he reads the Bible, he quoted a story from the very end of the Gospel of Luke: the road to Emmaus (Luke 24:13–35).

I think you should definitely read through the story if you have time, but I'll summarize it for you real quick. After Jesus died and rose again, He made lots of proof-of-life appearances to various followers. In one such moment, He joined a few of the early believers on a walk, though they didn't recognize it was Him. The two men were talking about what had happened to Jesus, discussing the tragic circumstances of His death and questioning the women's report that He had risen. It seemed like they'd given up on Him and decided He wasn't who they thought He was.

Jesus's response to their confusion and doubt is what I hope will echo in our minds every day as we dive into this study:

> *"Jesus said to them, 'Why are you so thick-headed? Why do you find it so hard to believe every word the prophets have spoken? Wasn't it necessary for the Messiah to experience all these sufferings and afterward to enter into his glory?' <u>And beginning with Moses and all the prophets he carefully unveiled to them the revelation of himself throughout the Scriptures.</u>"*
> Luke 24:25-27 TPT (emphasis added)

Jesus said that all of the Scriptures are about Him. And He wasn't referring to the four Gospels or to any of the other New Testament books—these hadn't been written yet! Jesus was saying that the Old Testament—that long collection of murky history, laws, and ominous prophecies—was intended to *unveil* Jesus to its reader.

Have you let that sink in? I can't help but align my hermeneutical thoughts right up with that pastor from TikTok. If Jesus said to read the Bible as though it's all about Him, then that's what I intend to do.

So, introducing *Most High: Reading 1 and 2 Samuel Like God is the Main Character.*

Our culture today is rabid for us to be the main character of our lives. "Me" is the lens through which we're urged to see the world. *Do what's best for me. Say no if it's not serving me. Only I can look out for me.* And, as cute and fun as it feels to savor our main-character moments, sometimes the "me" poison seeps into places it doesn't belong, even into the way we approach God's Word.

Let's just get it out there . . . A lot of us don't love reading the Old Testament. And most of the time, the reason we avoid it is because it's hard to find ourselves in it; it's hard to relate. But here's a news flash that has the potential to drastically change the way you approach Scripture: The Bible isn't about you. *It's about God!*

Jesus said that all of the Scriptures unveil His coming and His victory. And when we really and truly ascribe to that ideology, it becomes way less important if Old Testament books like Samuel, Chronicles, or Kings are "relatable" or not. They aren't self-help books intended to tell us how to win in our own twenty-first century ambitions. Instead, they are beautifully crafted, intentionally placed love letters to our Heavenly Father and Most High God. They are treasures woven together to chronicle the works and character of a living and breathing Savior, one who we can still abide in and interact with to this day.

We don't read the Bible to get to know ourselves better. We read the Bible to look at God.

That's our mission in this study as we dive into the books of 1 and 2 Samuel. We are cracking them open with honor and reverence, searching every line for glimpses of our King in Heaven and our risen Savior. And the crazy thing is when we take our eyes off ourselves and put them on God, somehow we find that something inside of us starts to change. As we learn about a God who hears us, we receive confidence to call out to Him. As we learn about a God who's intimate, we receive guidance on how to draw near to Him. As we learn about a God who's victorious, we learn how to experience that victory in our own lives.

God, in His kindness, turns a book about Himself into a blessing for us.

Do you want a closer look at that God? Are you sick of carrying the weight of being the center of your own universe? Are you craving a solid foundation of faith based on biblical truth, not rumors and guesses? Then join us as we turn our hearts to the Most High—the only One worth our attention, our worship, and our focus. Over the next ten weeks we will meet with a King who thunders from Heaven and a Father who sees our hearts. He will show us the beauty in the hard-to-understand and the glory in the mundane.

Imagine this study as a walk with Jesus along the road to Emmaus. He's showing us His story and unveiling His heart piece by piece. What an honor!

> *"The LORD thundered from heaven; the voice of the Most High resounded."*
> 2 Samuel 22:14

XOXO,
Maggie Sawler
Delight Ministries
Curriculum Development

Intro to Samuel

Why Samuel? It's a treasure hunt in a gold mine of glimpses of a Most High God!

Genesis/
Creation

Covenant with Abraham

Slavery in Egypt

Rescue & Exodus

Torah/Pentateuch/ Law

Key Themes
- God lifts up the humble and opposes the proud.
- God still works in spite of our brokenness.
- We are in desperate need of a Savior.

Fun Fact!
Did you know 1 + 2 Samuel were originally one book but were split when translated from Hebrew to Greek?

> Samuel tells the story of how a divided and tribal nation becomes the kingdom of Israel.

It all points to Jesus!

Promised Land — You are HERE!! — Kingdom of Israel — Babylonian Exile

History

Resources
- The Bible Project
- Enduring Word Commentary
- 1 and 2 Samuel for Everyone -John Goldingay
- 1 Samuel and 2 Samuel Bible Studies -John MacArthur

GOD WHO HEARS

MOST HIGH

God Who Hears

> Welcome to the very first chapter of our journey through the books of 1 and 2 Samuel! In this chapter we will dive into the story of Hannah and learn about the God who hears us and is present with us no matter what.

1 Samuel 1:1 - 2:11

I've done my fair share of crying out. I've tasted the desperation and the heartbreak that leads to prayer that softens the hardest heart, breaks down the tallest walls, and hopes to move the heart of God.

And part of me hopes you can't relate. There's a little corner of my spirit that wishes you didn't understand the kind of pain that leads to this depth of prayer and connection to the Lord. It's a part of me that still believes that easy is better and that God is in the light places more than the dark.

But I have a feeling you *do* know what this kind of crying out feels like. You know what a broken heart leads a weary soul to do. You know the kind of pain that wrings out your life and leads you straight to the feet of Jesus. It's the kind of pain that finally makes you realize you could never hope to handle it on your own—the kind that makes you realize God was your only option all along.

01 / GOD WHO HEARS

It's the kind of pain that leads you to grapple with this truth: *what if your story isn't about you, the one who cries out, but about God, the One Who Hears?*

Now, I feel a little bit inclined to apologize for starting this book off on such a heavy note. But ladies, we're about to study two books in the heart of the Old Testament. You've gotta face it now: *things are going to be heavy.* Think of this first chapter as your help in acclimatizing to the tone of 1 and 2 Samuel. It's a push into the deep end of the pool that helps your skin get used to the cold.

The lead-up to the books of Samuel helps us understand this heavy tone. Check out the very last line of the book of Judges, which chronologically comes right before Samuel:

> *"In those days Israel had no king;*
> *everyone did as they saw fit."*
> *Judges 21:25*

Pretty much, Judges is setting us up for some chaos. Everyone doing as they see fit sounds dangerous to say the least. It reminds me of the time I got stuck in a mob of people trying to cross a footbridge after a Taylor Swift concert. We all had individual places we needed to be and different plans for how to get there. There was pushing, shoving, crowding, squishing, and (mostly from me) crying. Now imagine that on a nationwide scale, and that's pretty much the state of the people of Israel as we enter into our study.

It's a cliff-hanger, a leading statement that makes you wonder if a king is coming and what it might mean for God's chosen people. And, spoiler alert, a king does come, but not in the way you might expect. Classic God move, right?

MOST HIGH

Quick Context!

The scroll of Samuel (originally one book that was later split into two parts) tells the story of the baby beginnings of the Israelite monarchy. Though named after the "Kingmaker" prophet and judge, Samuel, scholars don't agree on one author of the book. It records a crucial moment in the history of God's people, who had grown from one family into a nation freed from Egyptian slavery and finally residing in the Promised Land.

So, filled with tension, we pick up the storyline in 1 Samuel, and what do we find to kick off this chaotic and powerful tale of the long-awaited King of Israel?

We read the story of a woman who can't have children.

Buckle up because it's about to get wild.

Read 1 Samuel 1:1-18.

NOTES:

01 / GOD WHO HEARS

OK, we were just introduced to a lot of characters, so let's do a quick recap!

Elkanah	*The husband*
Hannah	*Wife #1 (childless)*
Peninnah	*Wife #2 (child-full)*
Eli	*Priest at Shiloh*

It reads a little bit like a soap opera. Elkanah, husband of the year, showed up to Shiloh to make one of the yearly sacrifices required by the Law (Deuteronomy 16:16–17). With him came Hannah and Peninnah, his two wives. And what do we learn about them?

Fill in the blanks from 1 Samuel 1:2.

"... Peninnah *had children, but* Hannah *had none.*"

For years, when they road-tripped to the tabernacle (the holy place where God's presence rested back in those days) for the sacrifice, Peninnah would torment Hannah about her lack of children. Again and again, she would remind her rival wife that she was blessed with sons and daughters while, "the LORD had closed Hannah's womb" (1 Samuel 1:6). We can imagine the strain on Hannah. Not only was her heart broken from that deep desire for children remaining unmet, but Peninnah was constantly rubbing salt in the wound.

MOST HIGH

We shouldn't be shocked that it led Hannah to cry out to the Lord.

> *"In her deep anguish Hannah prayed to the LORD, weeping bitterly."*
> *1 Samuel 1:10*

+ Can you think of the last time you cried out to the Lord like Hannah? What caused it?

> In life, looking at others girls I always want the relationships with their dad that I see. It pains me that I can't have it and seeing people posting it all on social media never helps.

The text goes on to say that Hannah was praying so fiercely and so intently that Eli, the priest on duty, thought she was *drunk*. Yikes! And Hannah's response to Eli's assumption hits our hearts even now, thousands of years later.

01 / GOD WHO HEARS

Fill in the blanks from 1 Samuel 1:15.

"'Not so, my lord,' Hannah replied, 'I am a woman who is deeply troubled. I have not been drinking wine or beer; I was pouring out my soul to the Lord.*'"*

God chose to begin the story of the rise of the kingship of Israel by telling us about a woman who *poured her soul out before the Lord*. I don't know about you, but that tells me a lot about the God I worship.

1. God hears us.

It would be so easy and natural to read this story and to see Hannah as the main character. Her story is so eye-catching and relatable! Who wouldn't gravitate to her? And to be honest, I've spent a lot of my time in the Word desperately trying to find myself in the characters, trying to relate to the lessons they were learning so that I could attempt to learn the same lessons. And I bet God loves that! He loves when we seek to understand His Word, without a doubt!

But something huge changed for me when I began to read the Bible like *God* was the main character of the story. You see, this isn't just a chapter about a woman in dire straits who cried out to God.

It's about the God who heard her.

MOST HIGH

I can't imagine that this was the first time Hannah had laid herself prostrate before the Most High in prayer. Likely, she had been pouring out her soul time and time again, begging God to intervene for her. Isn't that all of our stories, too? No way are we stopping at one prayer sesh for the thing that is heavy on our hearts and minds!

But how often do we feel like God stays silent, unmoved by our cries?

We beg God for miraculous healing, but that family member remains sick.

We pray again and again for our future husband, but we find ourselves back to square one after another terrible breakup.

We ask for freedom from the stress, anxiety, depression, or loneliness that plagues us, but then we wake up to another day with the same struggle.

It can be tempting to want to throw in the towel after the tenth, fiftieth, and thousandth time we've prayed the same prayer. I'm sure Hannah felt that way! But still, she poured her soul out to the Lord. Maybe she knew His character; maybe she knew that He could handle her honest feelings and frustrations.

It reminds us of Psalm 56 . . .

NOTES:

01 / GOD WHO HEARS

"You keep track of all my sorrows. You have collected all my tears in your bottle. You have recorded each one in your book."
Psalm 56:8, NLT

If we believe that God hears us—even when His answer to our cries is a closed womb like Hannah, another semester with that roommate, or a lost friendship—then our cries are never wasted. A God who hears keeps track of every tear; He leans in close with compassion.

I think there's something powerful to be found in the unity with the Father that happens when we're at the end of ourselves. Sister, you aren't just shouting to the void. God hears you, just as He heard Hannah all those years ago.

+ What's a prayer you've been praying lately that feels unanswered?

> I have been praying for God to ease my anxiety and urge to want to move home all become easier. But my anxiety gets worse, my urge to go home increases.

MOST HIGH

Our girl Hannah prayed with crazy persistence. And, miraculously, God came through for her.

> Read 1 Samuel 1:18-28.

> *"So in the course of time Hannah became pregnant and gave birth to a son. She named him Samuel, saying, 'Because I asked the L<small>ORD</small> for him.'"*
> *1 Samuel 1:20*

It's so important to embrace the fact that God doesn't always give us what we ask for. We are definitely called to pray without ceasing (1 Thessalonians 5:17) no matter the circumstance! But there's a really cool flip side to desperate prayer we often dare not explore.

Have you ever considered that God *wants* to come through for you?

01 / GOD WHO HEARS

2. God invites us to have faith that He will come through.

There are so many miracles in this first story of 1 Samuel, the most obvious being what we learned in verse 20. After years of crying out, God gave Hannah the baby she had been praying for! But there's another miracle hidden in these pages that feels just as powerful.

+ Reread 1 Samuel 1:17-18. Can you guess the miracle we're talking about?

> *The miracle that Hannah is having a baby*

The Word says that Hannah went away from the tabernacle, the place of her deep hurt and desperation, with a face no longer downcast. The New Living Translation says that "she was no longer sad." This is wild! *Before God gave her what she was asking for, she was cheered by the faith that He would come through.*

To fully flesh out this idea, we're going to need to jump around in our Bibles for a little, so hang with me here!

MOST HIGH

Fill in the blanks from   Matthew 21:22.

"If you <ins>believe</ins>, you will <ins>recieve</ins> whatever you ask for in prayer."

Now, fill in the blanks from   Psalm 37:4.

"Take delight in the Lord, and <ins>he will give</ins> you the desires of your heart."

OK, one more! Fill in the blanks from   Romans 8:28.

"And we know that in <ins>all thing</ins> God works for the <ins>good</ins> of those who love him, who have been called according to his purpose."

According to Scripture, God wants us to believe that He desires to give us what we ask for in prayer, all for our good and for His purpose and will. Now, this definitely doesn't mean that God gives us everything we want! That's a slippery thought pattern that will lead you to disappointment and disillusionment. But it does mean that you can have faith that He will come through for your good because that's His character!

Think about it like this. I'm one of those people who hates surprises. As much as I'd love to go with the flow, I've gotta admit that most of the time the flow needs to go with me. These control-freak tendencies really

01 / GOD WHO HEARS

got in the way when my now-husband and I began talking about getting engaged. I stressed about the time of year he would propose (it had to be summer so I had enough time to plan a wedding!). I stressed about who was going to be there when he proposed (did he know I wanted my family there?). I even stressed about how cute the proposal would be and if he would have a photographer there (did he even care about my Instagram aesthetic?). I nagged him, questioned him, and did my very best to ruin what should have been the biggest, most special surprise of my life.

Somehow, he pulled it off. The proposal was so special and so perfect—much sweeter than anything I could have tried to plan for myself. And looking back, I wish I had let go a little bit and trusted the man I loved. My husband is so sweet and so kind and so thoughtful! Why did I ever doubt that he would plan anything less than wonderful?

I knew he loved me and wanted what was best for me. I should have just trusted that he would come through!

Often, we're the same way with God. We get caught up in our asking and begging and planning and controlling that we forget to consider Who it is we're talking to. Of course a good God who loves us so much has good plans in store. Of course He cares about the desires of our hearts! Of course He is already at work, weaving a beautiful tapestry out of the threads of our lives, whether it looks how we expect it to or not.

How much happier would we be if we allowed that faith in His character to fill us up!? I don't know about you, but believing He'll come through sounds a lot more fun than dreading an inevitable letdown. Maybe we can walk away smiling like Hannah, even before the miracle.

THINK IT THROUGH!

+ Think back to the unanswered prayer you wrote about earlier. Be honest . . . Do you ever doubt that He will come through for you? Why or why not?

> I doubted myself more than God but every Sunday after church I would fell happier and calmer till I wasn't again

+ Are there any aspects of God's character you want to hold onto to build your faith in the waiting? Whether it's His goodness, His kindness, His peace, or His _____, write it down below to remind yourself of who He is!

> way of putting others first.

01 / GOD WHO HEARS

OK, let's wrap things up for this week! Go ahead and read 1 Samuel 2:1–11.

+ Did any of these verses stick out to you? Copy them down in the space below.

> "There is no one holy like the Lord; there is no one beside you; there is no Rock like our God
>
> 1 Samual 2:3
>
> (my handwring is too big)

At first glance, it might seem sort of random or unassuming, but Hannah's prayer of thanksgiving is so important for the rest of the books of Samuel.

It's not only her way of praising God for the miracle of her baby Samuel (who will become a key player in the story as we continue reading), but if you pay close attention to what she says, her prayer actually sets the tone for the rest of the narrative and hints at things to come.

So hang with us here, because we're about to zoom out and look at the big picture as we wrap up this chapter.

MOST HIGH

3. The Most High goes low... for you!

NOTES:

I learned I need to have no doubt in my prayer. It is just God and I against my anxiety. He is with me always. Focusing on my faith rather than negatives in my life can change everything ♡

If you've spent any period of time exploring the Bible, you've probably caught on to a certain theme. God consistently chooses the unexpected and the unlikely to be recipients of His grace.[1] He loves to challenge the status quo, flipping the world's expectations upside down and doing the opposite of what we might expect.

Hannah knew this about God!

01 / GOD WHO HEARS

"'The LORD brings death and makes alive; he brings down to the grave and raises up. The LORD sends poverty and wealth; he humbles and he exalts. He raises the poor from the dust and lifts the needy from the ash heap; he seats them with princes and has them inherit a throne of honor.'"
1 Samuel 2:6–8a

MOST HIGH

She experienced His upside-down grace in her own life when He showed favor and blessing to her in her lowest moments. And doesn't He do the same for us? He consistently meets us in the lowest places, bending down to offer us His hand when we need it the most. He bends down to hear us when we cry out and to strengthen us when we need more faith to get through. In fact, this willingness to meet His people where they're at is so integral to the character of God that it was on display in the most important moment in history.

+ Find Romans 5:8 and copy it down in the space below.

> "But God demonstrates his own love for us in this: while we were still sinners, christ died for us.

The Almighty, Most High God chose to humble Himself to death on a cross for you and me, the most unlikely and most unworthy. You see, this was always His character, even hundreds of years before Jesus was born! God's plan was always to make eye contact with us, His beloved creation, no matter the obstacles in the way.

In fact, if we read closely enough, we can see a hint of Jesus even here, in the prayer of a once-barren woman in a pre-monarchy Israel.

01 / GOD WHO HEARS

> "'He will give strength to his king and exalt the horn of his <u>anointed</u>.'"
> 1 Samuel 2:10b

+Look back at the verse above and underline "anointed."

Can you guess what the Hebrew word there is that we translate to "anointed"? *Messiah.*

God always planned to send a king to His people—yes, even these people who were living wildly and doing whatever they saw fit. But it wasn't going to be the king they expected or the story they had planned. He chose to use a mother's celebration to point to the coming Savior, the promised Messiah who would go to the lowest of lows for us.

As we continue reading in the books of 1 and 2 Samuel, I want to encourage you to keep your eyes open for a glorious God who chooses the humble for His mighty plans. We're going to see His character modeled time and time again in the midst of some crazy, tough, and heavy stories. Through it all, God stays true to who He is, offering us a clear perspective of the King we serve — the same King Hannah prayed to. He's the same God who invites us to cry out to Him and has the power to shine the light of hope in the darkest places.

Do you want to get to know the God Most High who hears your cries, rescues you from the depths, and raises you up in His arms? Then keep reading. He's got so much more in store for you.

CONVERSATION

1. Be honest. Is God the main character in your life these days? Why or why not?

> I wish he was. God gets my time but not enough. I say I am too busy but I should always have more time.

2. It can be hard to feel heard by God when our prayers feel unanswered. Can you think of a time in the past when God answered a prayer you prayed? What was it like?

> I prayed for God to lead me to the right thing when I was dealing with issues and God put the answers right in front of me.

STARTERS

3. God gives us the gift of faith in His character even in the waiting. Think about your unanswered prayer. Is there any way you feel called to change your attitude or perspective in the waiting?

> I needed to have hope that it would happen and remember things take time for everyone even God.

4. Let's vision cast! Spend some time in prayer, asking God to show you what He wants to teach you through this study. Compared to where you are currently at in your faith journey, where do you hope to be by the end of these ten weeks?

> I hope to be closer to God and figure out his word and how to be better with God

INTIMATE GOD

MOST HIGH

Intimate God

> Chapter 2, here we come! Last week we learned about the miracle baby who Hannah prayed for. Now, we get to continue on in the story and see how that baby shaped the future of the kingdom of Israel! God has so much in store for us as we learn His desire for intimate relationship with us. Let's jump in!

1 Samuel 3

Let's get super real here . . . Do you ever feel tempted to compare your time with the Lord to everyone else's?

Sometimes it feels like every time I open up my phone, I'm faced with another cutie patootie doing her morning quiet time in the most aesthetically pleasing way. She's got a wide-margin journaling Bible open on her sparkling countertop next to her professional-looking homemade latte with a huge candle that I can almost smell through the screen.

It's vibey. It's perfect. And I'm *jealous*. (Oof, please tell me I'm not alone in this!)

02 / INTIMATE GOD

I want to be like the other girls! I want the best quiet time setup known to man. I want the peaceful morning glow that would most certainly make it easier to focus on the ten chapters of the Word I plan to read that day. But when I was in college, my quiet time was spent next to a bowl of Froot Loops at my university-issued dorm desk in the semi-dark so I wouldn't wake my roommate up. That laser focus I expected was more like a groggy blur, letting my thoughts wander then trying to force them into submission so I could at least attempt to focus on my devo.

Can you relate? As Christians, we're told that time with God is critical and important, so we jump into it headfirst, only to find ourselves so caught up in the details and worrying if we're doing it right that we lose sight of why we're doing it in the first place. *How can we find true intimacy with God in our messy, chaotic, and confusing lives?*

I think this next portion of 1 Samuel has some answers for us. So let's dive in!

Read 1 Samuel chapter 3.

+ Have you read this story before? What stands out to you about it?

This is my first time reading this story

MOST HIGH

NOTES:

This story picks up in the life of Samuel, the baby Hannah prayed for. Once he was old enough, Hannah brought him back to the tabernacle at Shiloh to serve the Lord. Then, when he was around twelve years old, after ministering before the Lord for his whole life and learning priestly duties from Eli, God showed up in Samuel's life in a huge way.

Fill in the blanks from 1 Samuel 3:4a.

"Then the _Lord_ called _Samuel_."

This first truth is so simple yet has the power to change your whole life when it comes to your personal relationship with God. What if God is calling to you just as He called to Samuel?

1. God desires intimacy with us.

I grew up in a Christian home, learning about the Bible in school and Sunday school, filling my prayer journals up with lists of everyone I knew just to make sure I prayed for all of them. I had an *allegiance* to the Lord, but I don't think I had yet figured out that there was more to it than that. When I learned that God desired a *relationship* with me, so much changed.

02 / INTIMATE GOD

+ If you're honest, where's your faith at in this season? Rate where you are on the scale below. Are you more in allegiance to God or in relationship?

Allegiance — *Somewhere in the middle* — *Relationship*

I feel like I'm just going through the motions, and I get caught up in doing things for God.

Honestly, I'm not really sure where I'm at.

God and I are besties these days.

Intimacy with God can feel like such a vague concept. But in reality, it's as simple as twelve-year-old Samuel hearing the voice of God calling to him. We were made for an intimate, personal relationship with God—one with real conversations, real quality time, and real affection. Why? Because He loves us!

> *Flip all the way back in your Bible to Genesis 2 and skim through the scene.*

Intimacy was God's plan from the beginning. When He first created the world, He placed His humans in a beautiful garden. Then, He spent quality time with them! In Genesis 2 we see God growing trees with fruit that would please them, giving the man (Adam) a woman companion (Eve) so he wouldn't be lonely, and sitting with Adam while animals of every kind came by, just so Adam could name them. It's a picture of friendship, delight in each other, closeness . . . *intimacy!*

Even after the Fall (when Adam and Eve disobeyed God), we see a heartbreaking moment where God was walking in the garden, presumably waiting for His friends to join Him.

MOST HIGH

> *"Then the man and his wife heard the sound of the Lord God as he was walking in the garden in the cool of the day, and they hid from the Lord God among the trees of the garden. But the Lord God called to the man, 'Where are you?'"*
> *Genesis 3:8–9*

What unity He designed us for! Our God, the Most High King, wants to take walks with His beloved children in the cool of the day! He loves us so much that He desires intimacy with us, just as He desired intimacy with Samuel.

That's the kind of relationship with God I want—one where I can hear Him calling out to me and where I am ready to say, "Here I am!" But, if I'm honest, even when God is calling out to me, I'm not always in a position to listen—which leads us to our next point:

2. God speaks when we are in a position to hear.

Let's look back at the moment God called out to Samuel.

02 / INTIMATE GOD

+ **Look at 1 Samuel 3:3. Where was Samuel when God called out to him?**

> *He was lying in the house of the Lord*

God called to Samuel when he was in His presence, literally laying down to sleep in the House of the Lord, right by the Ark, which was the physical representation of God's presence in these pre-Jesus days. I don't know about you, but I want God to speak to me! So I will do anything I can to be in the best posture to hear His voice.

But how do we get practical with that? I mean, we can't exactly go lay down next to the Ark of the Covenant, right? Well, news flash: we don't have to! Thanks to Jesus's death and resurrection and the entrance of the Holy Spirit for believers in the book of Acts, we have free-range access to God's presence. He can be with us anywhere and everywhere! And in fact, as Christians, He's not just with us but He lives *inside of us!* So all we've gotta do is set our hearts to receive—to tune our ears to a God frequency.

One of our favorite ways to do this is through "quiet time." Contrary to popular belief, it doesn't have to be aesthetic or perfect or even necessarily quiet for God to show up. (Though if you are one of those aesthetic girlies, we applaud you!) *The point is to set your mind on God and posture your heart toward His.* Try playing some worship music, reading your Bible, or doing a devotional like this one. Create open space for prayer and quiet time to listen. It's there, in that posture in His presence, where God might just speak to you.

MOST HIGH

NOTES:

God is jealous of where we put our love somewhere that won't fulfill in a way He will

Now, we can tend to get frustrated if God doesn't holler at us with a, "Samuel, Samuel!" like He did in our Scripture reading. But God can speak to us in so many ways. Yes, sometimes it can be an audible voice, but it can more often be a sense of knowing in your spirit, a picture that pops in your head, or—our very favorite—a piece of Scripture that grabs your attention and says exactly what you need to hear.

And not only is this posture to hear a physical position (set apart time with your Bible and your focus on God) but it's also a response. If you want God to speak to you, He loves to move in a humble heart that's submitted to Him!

Think about Samuel again. Sure, He may have gotten a little confused by rushing to Eli first instead of God (we can cut him some slack—we would have been shook, too!), but his words teach us so much about the right posture to receive from God when He speaks.

> *"Then the L*ORD *called Samuel. Samuel answered, 'Here I am.' And he ran to Eli and said, 'Here I am; you called me.'"*
> *1 Samuel 3:4–5a*

02 / INTIMATE GOD

+ Look back at the verses on the page before and circle every time Samuel says, "Here I am."

Our boy Samuel's first response when God spoke to Him was humble availability. It's like He was saying, *Whatever you want from me, God, I'm here and I'm in. Whatever you want to say, I want to listen.*

We could spend a whole book researching this "Here I am" posture. In fact, it's just another installment in a long line of available responses from God's people.

> ## *Take it deeper!*
> Dig around in your Bible to check out other "Here I am" moments. Can you find any common themes?
>
> *Abraham, Genesis 22:1*
> *Jacob, Genesis 46:2*
> *Moses, Exodus 3:4*
> *Isaiah, Isaiah 6:8*
> *Ananias, Acts 9:10*

But for the sake of our conversation in this chapter, we've gotta get down to the meat: the Lord spoke to Samuel when he was in God's presence and when he was ready to submit himself to whatever the Lord might say. We can learn from that! Whether it's instituting a morning quiet time for the first time, engaging in more prayer throughout our days, or attending Sunday worship to get in God's presence, we can put ourselves in position to hear from the Lord. And, there, we can say, "Here I am," when He calls.

THINK IT THROUGH!

+ What does your time with the Lord look like these days?

> I spend my sundays with him and I try to talk to him at night and when anxios

+ Can you think of a time when God "spoke" to you? Maybe it was an audible voice, a feeling, a picture, or a Bible verse. Reflect on it below!

OR

Flip through your Bible and find a time God spoke to someone. What did He say? How did they respond?

> God told me to get involved with Him and the church more.

02 / INTIMATE GOD

OK, we have one more observation from Samuel's story to explore. Remember, this whole book is about letting God be the main character of the stories in 1 and 2 Samuel. So, yes, it's cool to learn from Samuel's posture, but there's something even sweeter when we look more closely at the God who calls Him.

I read this story and I see a God who's willing to break societal norms by speaking to a little kid when the prophetic voice had been silent for so long.

I see a God who isn't afraid to give His children hard assignments. (Did you read what God told Samuel when He finally got his attention? Yikes!)

I see a God who empowers the unlikely to do big things for His Kingdom and His plan.

But what strikes my heart right now is how God, our God, is patient enough to call out three times.

3. God is patient with us.

Reread 1 Samuel 3:2-10.

When we read the order of events here, it can feel a little funny. Sweet little Samuel is running around everywhere, trying to figure out who keeps calling out his name while he's trying to sleep. It's even funny that Eli, a seasoned priest, took so long to figure out what was happening. But finally, everything falls into place.

MOST HIGH

> *"The L*ORD *came and stood there,*
> *calling as at the other times, 'Samuel!*
> *Samuel!' Then Samuel said, 'Speak,*
> *for your servant is listening.'"*
> 1 Samuel 3:10

When I let it sink in, this really blows my mind. God had a message for Samuel, and an important one at that. He who had refrained from speaking to most of Israel (likely due to the wildness of their behavior at the time) finally spoke, and the person He spoke to didn't understand what was happening. He had to call out to Samuel three different times before he responded!

It comforts me that God would be patient enough with Samuel to give Him chance after chance to hear His voice because often I need Him to be patient with me, too.

I can think of times in my life when I begged God to give me an answer to a question that was heavy on my heart, but after months and months of crying out, I realized that in all my asking, I'd forgotten to actually listen for His voice. *Yet still He was patient with me.*

I've been at a worship night or church service when I clearly heard the Lord ask me to do something, then I spent weeks going back and forth trying to convince myself that He hadn't really spoken, mostly because I was scared to do what He was asking me to do. *Yet still He was patient with me.*

I've even given the same sin to Him over and over and over again, each time promising that this would be the last time. But then, I would do it again. *Yet still He was patient with me.*

02 / INTIMATE GOD

+ Can you relate? Think of a time when God was patient with you and write about it below.

> During my hardships with my dad and ex boyfriend when I let them treat me badly.

God's out-of-this-world, grace-filled patience even extends to this conversation about intimacy. I can imagine that so many of us who are reading this feel out of our depth and unqualified when it comes to intimacy with the Lord. Maybe you're the girl who's never tried to have a quiet time before, or you're the girl who keeps attempting to develop the habit but it never sticks. Or maybe you're the girl who hears stories about other people having crazy encounters with God and hearing His voice, but you feel like you're behind because you've never had a moment like this.

God is patient with you, too! Relationships don't develop overnight. Our best friends are our best friends because we've put time in getting to know each other, learning each other's hearts, and having fun together. It's the same way with God! The more time you spend getting to know Him, the deeper He lets you go and the more in love we become.

MOST HIGH

Fill in the blanks from Philippians 1:9-11.

"And this is my prayer: that your love may abound ___ and ___ in _____ and ___ of insight, so that you may be able to discern what is best and may be pure and blameless for the day of Christ, filled with the fruit of righteousness that comes through Jesus Christ—to the glory and praise of God."

These are some of my very favorite verses! Why? Because they say that we have room to *grow*!

Yes, God has designed us for intimacy and relationship with Him. Yes, He wants us to set aside time for Him. And yes, He wants us to posture ourselves to listen for His voice. But at the same time, He is a patient God who knows exactly where we're at and what's going on in our minds and hearts. He knows we need baby steps! He knows the things that take us extra time to understand and He knows the parts of ourselves we still feel tempted to hold back.

That's the beauty of our patient God. He loves you so much that He will keep coming back. He will keep knocking on the door of your heart. He will keep calling out your name.

So let today be the day that you shake off the fear of disappointing Him and the day that you finally decide you can't keep Him waiting any longer. Take that first baby step into intimacy with a trustworthy God who is ready to hold your hand every step of the way. Today, your love can abound more and more in knowledge and depth of insight. Today, you can be filled with the fruit of righteousness that comes through Jesus Christ (Philippians 1:9–11).

"The Lord was with Samuel as he grew up, and he let none of Samuel's words fall to the ground."
1 Samuel 3:19

*The same God who was with Samuel is with you.
Let's grab His hand and grow up together.*

CONVERSATION

1. Look back at the slider scale on page 45. Why did you answer that way? How do you want that relationship to grow or change?

> I want to grow with God because I feel like my best self with him.

2. "In what ways do you feel most intimate with God (e.g., on a walk in nature, listening to worship music, reading your Bible, journaling, etc.)?

> journaling makes me feel close to God and when I am at church

STARTERS

3. Samuel's "Here I am" was a posture of humble availability. Be honest . . . How do you think you would respond if God called your name like that? How can you begin to cultivate this posture of humble availability in your own life? In what areas of your life are you *not* humble or available these days?

> I would be happy to be called but wouldn't think I deserved it.

4. What does your "quiet time" with God currently look like? (Flip back to the *Think It Through* section for help!) What do you want it to look like? What action steps can you take to implement that vision? [HINT: Write down the ideas your small group members share for inspiration!]

> music and journaling and prayers

JEALOUS GOD

MOST HIGH

Jealous God

> *Chapter 3 is finally here! Join us for some intense Bible study and hard convos as we read about King Saul and learn more about God's jealousy and what it means for our lives.*

1 Samuel 8 – 10 & 1 Samuel 15

Alright ladies! We gotta crack our knuckles, stretch out our muscles, and buckle in for this chapter because we are about to do some serious Bible study. This week we're covering the rise and fall of Saul, the first ever king of Israel. It's going to be a character study that spans a fairly large chunk of Scripture (think high school English class)—but we're not studying the character you might think!

I mean, sure, we could spend a whole chapter deep-diving into Saul's character, but I've gotta say . . . It sounds like a much better use of our time to deep-dive into *God's* character. As we watch our God interact with little ole Saul, we can learn a lot about who He is and how He desires to interact with us.

First, let's do a quick recap! Last week we left off with Samuel as a little twelve-year-old just learning how to hear God's voice. Over the course of the next few chapters, we see Samuel blossom into a well-respected prophet and judge as he takes over for the OG priest, Eli, who made some

03 / JEALOUS GOD

bad decisions and ended up literally dying from shock at the sin of the Israelites he was supposed to be leading. Samuel swoops in to save the day with a beautiful speech inviting God's people to turn their hearts back to the Lord and, for a time, they do.

But, as we've come to expect from these biblical characters, their God-focus eventually goes off-track. And that's where we pick up in 1 Samuel chapter 8.

Read 1 Samuel 8:1-9.

+ Summarize what you just read in the space below.

Suddenly, after so many years as the nation of Israel, God's people demanded a king. And *why* did they demand a king? To be "like all the nations" (vs 5). Yikes. To really understand the magnitude of this moment, we need to hop back in time for a second.

MOST HIGH

+ Flip to Judges 8:22–23. Who did Gideon say would rule over Israel?

This was always the deal for the chosen people of God. God was in charge. He was their ruler. He was always the king they needed, just as He still is for us today. God always designed us to only look to Him.

1. God is a jealous God.

If you run in Christian circles, you've probably heard God described this way before. But in our modern context, it can feel a little weird. What does it even mean for God to be jealous? Is He envious of something?

If you flip through your Bible, you will actually find a *lot* of verses that describe God as jealous. Essentially, we can define His jealousy as His uncompromising commitment to the right placement of honor, worship, and affection, especially as it applies to the hearts of His beloved children. In my research for this chapter, I was shocked at how many times it comes up in Scripture! Clearly, this is an important attribute of God's character.

03 / JEALOUS GOD

Take it deeper!

Here are just a few of the many verses that talk about the jealousy of God. Check them out!

Exodus 34:14
2 Corinthians 11:2
Deuteronomy 6:15
Deuteronomy 5:9
Nahum 1:2
Isaiah 42:8
Ezekiel 39:25

Think back to the book of Exodus and God's introduction of the Ten Commandments to the people of Israel. What was the very first command He gave?

+ Flip to Exodus 20 and copy commandment number one in the space below. (Hint: Check verse 3.)

MOST HIGH

You see, <u>God is jealous because He wants our full attention, allegiance, and love</u>. He is not interested in sharing His children with lesser "gods" that will never provide for them, care for them, or lead them like He can. He is a *consuming fire* (Deuteronomy 4:24) because He created us to be with Him and for Him, subjects to His rule, sheep in His pasture, and friends of His heart. He is the only one who can capture our attention, burning so bright we cannot help but keep our eyes focused on Him.

So when He says that we shall have no other gods before Him, He means it. According to God, He is the one true King. No one and nothing else will do.

And that's where the Israelites go wrong in 1 Samuel 8. God, obviously aware of what's going on, explains it to a very distressed Samuel.

Fill in the blanks from 1 Samuel 8:7–8.

"And the LORD told him: 'Listen to all that the people are saying to you; it is not you they have rejected, but they have _____ me as their _____. As they have done from the day I brought them up out of Egypt until this day, _____ me and serving other ___, so they are doing to you.'"

03 / JEALOUS GOD

God knows the people are rejecting His leadership by asking for a king. And, as we keep reading in the chapter (read 1 Samuel 8:1–21 for context), He knows the consequences of that kind of request. I read in a book once that we need to be careful what we beg God for because we run the risk of getting exactly what we ask for.[1] The poor Israelites are about to face that risk as the story continues.

It's so important that we lay the groundwork here before we continue reading about these people who rejected God's kingship and asked for a king of their own. Because, as much as we hate to admit it, we do the exact same thing in our own lives daily.

God is still jealous for us today. He is jealous for our time, but we spend it on everything else but Him. He is jealous for our attention, but we go weeks forgetting to talk to Him.

He is jealous for our allegiance, but we serve the little gods of social media, substance, romance, and success as if they are worthy of our everything.

I think it can be easy to disqualify ourselves from this conversation because we voted for a politician in the election last year, not a king to fight our battles with sword and armor. But I think this is one of the most relevant conversations we've ever had in a Delight study.

Your God is a jealous God. What does that really mean to you?

+ Quick recap before we keep moving! In your own words, what does it mean that God is a jealous God?

> *He is jealous of where we are putting our love when it doesn't give the same love*

MOST HIGH

Now it's time for Saul, the king the Israelites asked for, to enter the picture. In the text, there are two different versions of Saul's rise to power. I like to think of them as his secret anointing (1 Samuel 9:1–10:16) and his public anointing (1 Samuel 10:17–27).

The first "secret" anointing story is *wild*. Please go read it in your own time! Basically, Saul runs into Samuel while on a hunt for some missing donkeys, and God tells him to anoint the Benjaminite young man as king. There are some fun antics, but ultimately God gives Saul sign after sign that He had chosen him to lead His people. But the people didn't know it yet.

And that's where we pick up in the "public" anointing story.

> *Read 1 Samuel 10:17–27.*

+ Based on your reading, how would you describe Saul?

It's a scene worthy of an HBO Max series. The Israelites pull a handsome, tall guy out of a pile of boxes (where he had been literally hiding from them), and they scream, "Long live the king!" We can picture Samuel, who didn't even want to anoint a king anyway, giving some jazz hands and saying, "Ta-da!" If I'm being honest, it doesn't sound like the most auspicious start to a kingdom. It's giving . . . hot mess.

03 / JEALOUS GOD

But remember who we're looking to as we read! Even here, in the chaotic weirdness that is these few chapters of 1 Samuel, we can see God's heart and character at work. Even in the mess, God has *compassion*.

2. God has compassion on us even when we reject Him.

I have a five-year-old, twenty-pound puppy named Rosie at home, and she is the cutest little sinner I know. Just the other day, we discovered she has a passion for frisbees. And when I say passion, I mean an *obsession*. She can't get enough of it! We throw it for her in the backyard and she literally yelps with delight. But the issue is, she's not the most well-behaved frisbee player. When we throw it for her, she takes it and runs, doing everything she can to never have to return it to our hands (yes, with lots of growling and snarling involved). She sits by the back door every day and cries, both eyes glued to the frisbee we "hid" on the fireplace mantle. She point-blank refuses to go outside without the frisbee.

Now, a part of me wants to throw that frisbee away because I'm sick of her attitude. If I have to pry that plastic thing from her jaws one more time, I might lose my mind. But there's another part of me that can't help but smile every time she chases after it with her little legs. I love that she loves it! I love to know that we're making her happy. I love that this eight-dollar toy brings her so much joy, even though she can't quite handle it the way we want her to.

MOST HIGH

And I can't help but wonder if that's sort of how God feels about the Israelites in these moments we're reading about. He loves them so much that He wants to provide for them and supply their every need. But He sees the underlying sin that causes them to reject His guidance and leadership. He watches them foam at the mouth for their frisbee (king Saul), and He can't help but show them compassion, even when He knows they can't handle what they're asking for.

Fill in the blanks from 1 Samuel 9:16.

"About this time tomorrow I will send you a man from the land of Benjamin. Anoint him ruler over my people Israel; he will deliver them from the hand of the Philistines. I have looked on my people, for their ____ ____ ____ ____."

They were crying out for the wrong thing and actively rejecting God as their king, but still He heard them and had compassion on them. Even when they were actively running away from Him, like Rosie with her frisbee, God chose to move on their behalf. He even had compassion on the one He chose to anoint as their king! Think about it. Saul was just this normal guy from a not-so-great tribe who was so scared of leadership that he hid from the people who would crown him. But still, God reached His hand down and raised him up. Even knowing the tumultuous times ahead for the Israelites and the sin Saul would fall prey to, He still gave him the chance to step up.

We can't look to God as jealous and forget about His compassion. He's not just one or the other! Always and in every moment, God is *both*.

03 / JEALOUS GOD

Even when He was on the cross, actively being rejected, tortured, and murdered, Jesus's inclination toward His people was compassion.

> *"Jesus said, 'Father, forgive them, for they do not know what they are doing.'"*
> Luke 23:34a

Does it blow your mind to consider that God would have the same compassion toward you? Is it possible that He doesn't just love you when you're doing great, walking in the light and making the right decisions? What if He loves you just as much when you're in your room falling into that secret porn addiction? What if He loves you just as much when you wake up hungover in a stranger's bed? What if He loves you just as much when you sleep through church for the third week in a row or when you lie to your professor?

What if He loved you just as much before you ever even gave your heart to Him?

We reject and reject and reject the God who should be our only love. But still, He reaches out His hand in compassion.

THINK IT THROUGH!

+ What is the "king" in your life that has taken your eyes off of God? It could be a dream, a sin pattern, a person, or a struggle. Name it here.

+ Be honest. Is it hard to accept God's compassion in your rejection? Why or why not?

03 / JEALOUS GOD

This Scripture has already wrecked me, but somehow we're not done yet! We have one last moment in Saul's story to explore. And, unfortunately, it's his failure.

Read 1 Samuel 15. (We know it's a lot, so take notes in your Bible as you go to help keep it all in your brain!)

In between his anointing and chapter 15, Saul has been busy doing kingly things. He's out fighting and winning battles with his son Jonathan, and for a little while it seems like his kingship might be a good thing for the Israelites. But then pride sneaks in and Saul forgets who raised him up in the first place. The story we read in chapter 15 is the second installment of Saul's disobedience and the final straw for God and Samuel. If we're viewing Saul's life and reign as a rollercoaster, it's all downhill from here.

God asks Saul to completely destroy a neighboring kingdom called the Amalekites. (These guys were bad news, evil to the core.) So Saul, high on military victory and over-confident by this point, marches to battle against them. But he doesn't do what God told him to do.

+ Reread 1 Samuel 15:7–9. What did Saul and the army do wrong?

MOST HIGH

Instead of obeying God's command to wipe out the Amalekites and all their property, Saul chooses to save "the best" for himself. Obviously, God is not cool with it and Samuel has to confront the king.

Samuel finds Saul near a monument he had set up for himself (red flag), and it is obvious Saul has no remorse for his actions and honestly seems unconvinced that he had done anything wrong. Samuel has to call him out.

> "'Why did you not obey the LORD? Why did you pounce on the plunder and do evil in the eyes of the LORD?'... 'To obey is better than sacrifice, and to heed is better than the fat of rams. For rebellion is like the sin of divination, and arrogance like the evil of idolatry. Because you have rejected the word of the LORD, he has rejected you as king.'"
> 1 Samuel 15:19; 22b-23

Oof. It's a brutal message. The one God had chosen to be His representative to the people–His anointed–had turned around and rejected God. In his disobedience, Saul stepped out of the favor God had on his life. It's a tough pill to swallow, but we can't wrap this chapter up without facing it. We serve a God who asks for our obedience.

03 / JEALOUS GOD

3. God delights in obedience.

In my time as a Christian, I've heard God described in so many ways. I've heard the sermons that were biblical beatdowns, filled with shame and condemnation for those who mess up. But I've also heard the mushy messages that speak only of God's kindness and grace, almost painting Him as a pushover who's cool with whatever.

+ Which message do you feel like you hear more often? How do you think that affects the way you relate to the Lord?

It stirs a question in our hearts: could God be different, more complex, than we thought?

Even now as I write this, I feel weird bringing up the idea of obedience and disobedience. Can't we just leave it at compassion? But this tension is the

MOST HIGH

push and pull present in every Christian's heart. We are called to love God *and* to obey Him. He delights in our affection and in our obedience. We can't just choose one and ignore the other!

Look back at verse 23. What was Saul's disobedience in God's eyes? *Idolatry*.

Saul's disobedience betrayed his heart. Instead of turning his eyes toward God, he turned inward and outward, trying to please himself and to please the people. He put himself on the throne (literally and figuratively) and decided to do what he thought was best, ignoring the clear instructions from God. It all goes back to the beginning of his reign. The Israelites rejected God, so they asked for a king. The king rejected God, so he disobeyed.

But God is a jealous God. He can't be cool with idols. *He's always got to tear them down!*

That's why God loves our obedience! Obedience knocks down idols and exalts God! Every single time we choose to obey God's commands over our own wants and desires, it's like we're telling God He's the King in our lives. It's little moments and huge moments where we get to look our Father in the eyes and tell Him that He's more important than our earthly desires and plans. Every act of obedience is an act of love that delights the heart of the King we were designed to worship.

It's a shift in perspective! What if obedience wasn't drudgery but a joy? Every time we choose to speak life over a friend instead of gossip, we're loving God. Every time we honor our parents instead of blowing up on them, we're loving God. Every time we say no to that temptation, we're loving God.

03 / JEALOUS GOD

You see, when you know your Father, *when you really know Him,* you get to do what pleases Him! You become familiar with His heart, and you can't help but get closer and closer. Suddenly, His kingship in your life is second nature, and His compassion overflows into everything you do. In fact, His desire for obedience starts to feel like another way He shows His compassion toward you—a protection and a guide rail for life. And when you know that He loves your obedience, it's not a chore anymore. It's a joy!

In the next chapter, God is going to anoint a new king, one He describes as a man after His heart. But this new king isn't better because He never sins or slips into disobedience. In fact, the new king will mess up just as much as Saul. But the difference is that he consistently chases after the heart of God. I don't know about you, but that's who I want to be! I want to look back on my life and say with joy that though I messed up time and time again, I never stopped chasing after the heart of God. Let the new revelations of His character we learned this week draw you closer to Him.

Allow God to show you His jealousy and His compassion, His desire for your obedience and His desire for your love.

There is no other King for me but Jesus.

NOTES:

CONVERSATION

1. What feelings does the idea of God's jealousy and His desire for obedience bring up in your heart? Discomfort? Confusion? Sadness? Why do you think that is? How does it affect the way you view God?

> I used my negative views of jealously

2. Think back to the "king" in your life that takes your eyes off God. What would it look like to lay it down at His feet? What would surrender look like in that area?

STARTERS

3. Can you think of a time when you saw the compassion of God at work in your life or in the life of someone around you? What was it like?

4. God *delights* in our obedience! What is one area in your life you feel called to walk in obedience with after reading this chapter?

GOD WHO SEES

MOST HIGH

God Who Sees

> We're slowing things down a little bit this week (can I get an amen!?) to study just thirteen verses of one famous story. As we read about the anointing of David, we'll get to learn about God's gaze and what it means that He sees us. Are you ready? Let's do this!

1 Samuel 16:1 – 13

I'm not going to lie . . . I am so excited about this chapter!

I feel a little bit like my grandpa. I have so many fond memories of sitting on his lap in his recliner that had towels on each of the arms (still not 100 percent sure why) and listening as he read me book after book. His voice was better than any audiobook narrator, bringing classic stories alive as he turned the pages of picture books his mom had read to him as a kid, their pages cracked and yellow.

This week's story from Scripture is *gold*. It's a classic, passed down from generation to generation. It's a story I am so excited to open up in front of you and watch as you breathe it in. God has something so special and so unique to speak to you this week through His Word! I believe it in my bones.

This week is for the girl who needs to know how God sees her because she can't look in the mirror anymore. It's for the girl who's always felt like the ugly one, the broken one, or the one who doesn't fit in. It's for the girl who feels unnoticed by everyone, even God.

04 / GOD WHO SEES

Your God sees you. And He sees you differently than how you see yourself. *What a relief!*

> Read 1 Samuel 16:1–13.

Alright, we need to grab some context real quick because this little piece of Scripture literally sets the tone for the whole Bible. I'm giving you some bullet points of the biggest things to remember below to refer back to as you read.

Anointing: In the Old Testament, people and things were anointed to signify that they were being set apart for God. Just like Saul was set apart and chosen as the next king of Israel, so was David. The horn God talks about in verse 1 is likely a ram's horn holding a type of scented olive oil. The horn is significant because it symbolizes victory (think of a bull goring its enemy with its horn, thus becoming victorious). If you think back to Hannah's prayer in 1 Samuel 2, you'll see that she references the horn in verse 10.

Jesse of Bethlehem: David's family is significant to the storyline of the Bible in a lot of ways. First of all, Jesse was actually the grandson of Ruth and Boaz, whose story you can read in the book that comes right before 1 Samuel. And, if you've spent much time in the New Testament, you'll probably recognize "Bethlehem" as the birthplace of Jesus! Jesus's lineage being from the line of David is super critical to His story, so it is so cool to see the beginnings of that lineage here!

Saul: We read last week that King Saul had stepped out of the favor of God, prompting God to find a new king who would be after His heart, as Saul had chosen to lead out of selfish ambition. But the Israelites didn't know about all this going on behind the scenes between Samuel and Saul and God. So this anointing of David—the new king—had to be super secretive. Keep that in mind as we read. Just because David gets anointed doesn't mean he gets to lead right away. For all intents and purposes, Saul was still in charge.

MOST HIGH

The story starts off with a command. God tells Samuel to go off in search of a new king to replace the one who had turned his back on the Lord. Samuel sets out with lots of faith and a horn full of oil, trusting that God will guide him as the future of Israel hangs in the balance.

> *"... I will show you what to do. You are to anoint for me the one I indicate."*
> 1 Samuel 16:3

When Samuel arrives in Bethlehem, he invites the family of Jesse to a sacrifice, the perfect way to scope out the options. And apparently Samuel thought it was going to be easy because right as Eliab—who we assume to be the firstborn—struts in, Samuel declares, "Surely this is the dude!" But God had something different in mind, and the wisdom in His answer reverberates in our hearts even today, thousands of years later.

Fill in the blanks from 1 Samuel 16:7.

"But the LORD said to Samuel, 'Do not consider his **appearence** or his height, for I have rejected him. The LORD does not look at the things people look at. **People** look at the outward appearance, but the **Lord** looks at the **♡**.'"

I don't know about you, but I think this verse alone has the potential to change my life.

1. God looks at your heart.

04 / GOD WHO SEES

I had a pastor tell me once that this verse was a double whammy. It doesn't just teach us that God is interested in our hearts, but it also *warns* us that people get caught up in outward appearance. And boy, isn't that the truth!

As much as some of us hate to admit it, I think we all are a little bit (or a lotta bit) caught up in the way we look. We use apps to edit our Instagram posts to make our teeth look whiter, we spend more money on skincare and shampoo than we care to admit, and we meticulously plan our outfits for church the night before. And that's not always a bad thing! Our bodies are temples of the Holy Spirit, of course we want to make them pretty!

But the bad thing is the poison that seeps into our brains when appearance takes the front seat. I think you know the feeling I'm talking about. It's that little voice whispering in your ear that you're ugly, you're dirty, you're not enough . . . Even now you can probably hear it. Your own brain calls you names, whether we say them out loud or we harbor them inside and secret.

Gosh, I've been through seasons where I actually *hated* myself and the way I look. And I know I'm not alone. It's a toxic thought pattern all revolving around the person in the mirror that holds us captive.

I know we have all heard so many cheesy lines saying, "God made you beautiful," and, "You're perfect just the way you are," so I'm not even going to go there. What if we can take a different approach with all this? Instead of looking at this like we're the main character trying to fix the way we look at ourselves, let's look at God and what He says and what He sees and what's important to Him.

> *"but the LORD looks at the heart."*
> 1 Samuel 16:7b

MOST HIGH

God just isn't as interested in the way we look as we are. It's weird to think about, but it's true! Earthly accolades and beauty in the eyes of others are actually fairly low on God's priority list. In fact, did you know that Jesus wasn't pretty?

> *"He grew up before him like a tender shoot, and like a root out of dry ground. <u>He had no beauty or majesty to attract us to him, nothing in his appearance that we should desire him.</u> He was despised and rejected by mankind, a man of suffering, and familiar with pain. Like one from whom people hide their faces he was despised, and we held him in low esteem."*
> Isaiah 53:2-3 (emphasis added)

This verse in Isaiah is literally describing Jesus, Savior of the world and God as man, and it pretty much says that He wasn't attractive. Y'all, I'm not making this up! Did you know that the New Testament has no physical description of Jesus? We have no clue how tall He was, how straight His teeth were, or what His hair type was. It just wasn't an important detail to God that needed to be written down for posterity. (Though in Heaven, we know Jesus got a major glow up that included wool-hair and fire-eyes. Check out the book of Revelation if you're curious!)

God's just not interested in appearance. He looks deeper. He's interested in our *hearts*. What a correction! Yes, He speaks so tenderly to us when we feel less-than and when the mirror floods us with lies, but He also asks us to redirect our focus to what He's focusing on! He would much prefer a humble heart over a pretty face.

I can almost picture Him standing over my shoulder as I'm looking in the mirror. *Look at me,* He says. And honestly, I'd much rather give Him all my attention and let Him work on my heart than keep trying to learn how to curl my hair to keep up with the trends.

THINK IT THROUGH!

+ **What do you think God loves most about your heart?**

> I think God loves how kind and forgiving I am. I always give the benefit of the doubt

+ **What aspect of your appearance tries to steal your attention away from God?**

> I think my own head takes my time from God because it's always spinning

MOST HIGH

OK, let's keep going! Our favorite story just keeps getting better and better.

Read 1 Samuel 16:8–11.

I'm not the pretty sister.

Now, if you know me, you know that I love my sister more than pretty much everyone else. She's my person, the gal I would do anything for. But since she hit puberty, it's become common knowledge that she is the "pretty sister." It started innocently with all of our extended family and friends commenting on how she was growing into such a beautiful young woman, but eventually it grew to a line in the sand. She got the pretty genes while I, unfortunately, did not.

I pride myself on being someone who doesn't really care what people think of me. I don't remember struggling with body image issues growing up; I guess I just always assumed I was cute because my mom said so. But as my sister became gorgeous, I found myself staring at her Instagram pictures and wondering why mine didn't look like that. I asked for her makeup routine on the sly and wondered what diet she was on to get her body to grow that way when mine just didn't.

I even asked her once, *Why are you so much prettier than me? Aren't we supposed to look alike?* When she replied that it was something about my bone structure, I found myself staring at my face in every mirror I walked by, hyper-analyzing my jaw line.

And I can't help but think of this when I read about Samuel going through brother after brother. I feel the sibling rivalry bubbling in my bones. But it really all boils down to one thing: *comparison.*

04 / GOD WHO SEES

2. God calls you uniquely.

Fill in the blanks from 1 Samuel 16:11.

"So he asked Jesse, 'Are these all the sons you have?' 'There is still the **youngest**,*' Jesse answered. 'He is tending the sheep.' Samuel said, 'Send for him; we will not sit down until he arrives.'"*

There are so many layers to this! You can see it from Samuel's perspective: he was comparing brother to brother, choosing the tallest, the oldest, or the most "kingly" looking. Or you can see it from Jesse's perspective: he put the most likely sons in front of Samuel—he thought them much more qualified for such distinguished company than the youngest son who hadn't even been invited to dinner. You can even see it from David's perspective: it must have felt pretty sucky to be left out in the fields with the sheep when all your brothers got to attend the party of the year.

But from God's perspective . . . He wasn't sorting through brother after brother trying to pick the best. He knew who He was calling.

We've seen time and time again this theme in the books of Samuel where God chooses the least likely for His big purposes, and this was no exception! David was so unlikely he wasn't even given a place at the table! But God wasn't searching through the masses. He found the one He'd already chosen and purposed for His plan.

MOST HIGH

Isn't He the same God now? While we're caught up trying to look like the girl in our eight a.m. class, trying to *not* look like the basic gals, and trying to distinguish ourselves for our professors for a grade, our pastors for a job, or a boy for attention, God was never putting us in a category with anyone else.

He made you *you*. Why would anyone else matter?

Now I know this might feel like common sense, but it's such an important reminder! If we're trying to catch the way God sees us, we have to know that He's not seeing us through the filter of the people around us. When God looks at us, He sees the individual He created for His pleasure and purpose. Even further, the Bible says that when you give your life to Jesus you become "hidden with Christ in God" (Colossians 3:3). So, technically, when God looks at you He sees the finished work of Jesus Christ in you and on you and all around you.

We are each specially made for a unique purpose that was ordained, chosen, and set into motion by the King of the world. I don't know about you, but I don't want to waste my time comparing myself to everyone else. I want God to have full permission to captivate my attention. He waits for me to go where He's leading and to accept His call so He can anoint my head with oil. And He "will not sit down until [I] arrive" (1 Samuel 16:11).

+ Think about it . . . How big of a struggle is comparison in your life these days? What aspect of your life is the easiest for you to compare to others?

> I compare everyday, how I don't look or act the same. The easiest thing to compare is my looks and way of life.

04 / GOD WHO SEES

Alright, we gotta wrap this up. Let's focus in on the last part of our story.

Reread 1 Samuel 16:12-13.

+ What stands out to you the most from these two verses?

> when the Lord says "Rise and annoint, this is the one".

Teenage David finally comes onto the scene, "glowing with health," and God pokes Samuel on the shoulder to tell him this is the one they'd been waiting for

> "So Samuel took the horn of oil and anointed him in the presence of his brothers, and from that day on the Spirit of the LORD came powerfully upon David. Samuel then went to Ramah."
> 1 Samuel 16:13

MOST HIGH

It's one of those biblical moments that feel like they need to be accompanied with a full orchestra and dramatic lighting. David (*the* King David, superstar) is finally anointed as king of Israel. And, my very favorite part, *the Spirit comes upon Him.*

+ Look back at the verse on the page before and underline "the Spirit of the Lord came powerfully upon David."

3. The best thing about you is God's Spirit in you.

This is the start of something huge for David and for the nation of Israel. David (spoiler alert) goes on to slay a giant, win countless military victories, reign over a unified Israel, establish the capital city of Jerusalem, and found a dynasty that will leave a permanent mark on the history of the world and, eventually, pave the way for the birth of a Savior.

And all of this happens to and through a little shepherd boy. How? Why? *Because the Spirit of God came powerfully upon him!*

This whole chapter really has turned into a discussion on identity. How does God see us when we feel ugly and unnoticed? How does God feel about us when we get caught up in the crowd? But the secret to identity—a secret we can so clearly see in the pages of Scripture—is that we are founded in the Spirit of God. What makes me *me* and what makes you *you* is God in us. He is the best thing about us, the only thing worthy of note.

04 / GOD WHO SEES

Fill in the blanks from 2 Corinthians 1:21-22.

"Now it is **God** *who makes both us and you stand firm in Christ. He* **anointed** *us, set his* **seal** *of ownership on us, and put his* **Spirit** *in our hearts as a deposit, guaranteeing what is to come."*

God makes us stand firm. God anoints us. God seals us as His. God puts His Spirit in us. And that's the key to knowing who you are and whose you are and why you're here!

David wasn't impressive because he was handsome and glowing with health. He was impressive because of *God's Spirit in Him.*

You aren't beautiful because you found the best concealer and the newest hair oil. You are beautiful because of *God's Spirit in you.*

You aren't chosen for your unique calling because you proved yourself worthy. You are chosen because of *God's Spirit in you.*

You aren't going to Heaven because you do everything right. You are going to Heaven because of *God's Spirit in you.*

What an answer to that craving in our hearts for affection, attention, and approval! Suddenly, the weight is off our shoulders. It's not on us to be anything. It's all about God! I am not the main character of my life. *God is!*

The anointing of David paints a beautiful picture of the character of God. He's the One who sees the far off, unlikely one and raises him up. I wish I could have been there!

MOST HIGH

It must have been such a holy moment, to feel the hand of God as He set His plan in motion to rescue His people. Apparently David felt like it was a big moment because he actually memorialized it in a Psalm. (Did you know, on top of everything else, David also wrote a huge chunk of the book of Psalms? OK, overachiever!) This Psalm is where we're going to land for this week's chapter.

Turn in your Bible to Psalm 23 and read it a few times.

Do you have goose bumps like I do? How cool is it that we get an even closer glimpse at this historical moment!? Seeing it from David's perspective really solidifies everything we've been learning.

Look at it one more time. Do you see who the focus is on?

+ With your Bible open to Psalm 23, circle every time it references God doing something (e.g., you, the Lord, He, etc.).

God led Him to the right place. *God* refreshed him. *God* was with him. *God* comforted him. *God* gave him a seat at the table. *God* anointed him. *God* committed to walking with him for the rest of his life.

You see, the more I think about God, the less I think about me.

When I know He sees me, I don't need anyone else to.

When I know how He sees me, I don't need to look down on myself.

When I know He sees me as if I'm the center of His world, I don't need to look at anyone else.

04 / GOD WHO SEES

When I know that thanks to the work of Jesus Christ on the cross, I am host to the Spirit of the living God, I don't have to strive.

It's all *God*.

Let this Scripture preach a new word to your heart this week. Whether you're the least likely brother, you're waiting for your anointing, or you're caught up in the mirror, ask God for the beautiful refresh you've been waiting for.

He sees me. So all I see is Him.

NOTES:

I love how God sees all of us as the best. Not just certain parts of us but all of us.

CONVERSATION

1. Let's start this off with a basic reflection question. Did you learn something new this week about the Bible, God, or yourself? What was it?

> I learned how God will always love me and never compare me to others like I do myself

2. What's your favorite thing about yourself and the way God made you? What part of yourself do you struggle the most to love? Why do you think that is?

> I love how God put my struggles and hardship of my life into the best of me to make me better.

STARTERS

3. Is there something unique you feel like God has anointed you to do? What is it? How do you feel called to step out more confidently in that calling?

> To not be afraid of hard things because they shape me into who I am

4. Which verse from Psalm 23 stands out to you the most in this season in your life? Why?

> "He refreshes my soul."

05

GOD OF VICTORY

MOST HIGH

God of Victory

> *How are we already half way through our study of 1 and 2 Samuel? God has been moving through His Word these past few weeks, and He has something special in store for this chapter. Welcome to Invitation Week, a beloved Delight tradition where we make eye contact with Jesus as He invites us to give our lives to Him.*

1 Samuel 17

I used to believe that the peak of the Christian life was battle-free.

Thinking back, what I would have defined as the most "fruitful" seasons of my life were the easy seasons, the sweet seasons. When I walked pretty paths and felt the sun on my face and succeeded in everything I tried, I believed that God was with me there. He was pleased with me, so He rewarded me. He liked what I had done, so He gave me a soft place to lay my head.

Those were the days when I believed that battles were something you could choose to walk in or out of. Bad decisions or a weak mind led me into hard places, and wisdom and Scripture memorization led me out. My Jesus was sugar-sweet and surface-level, waiting on the mountaintop for me to get my act together and meet Him there.

05 / GOD OF VICTORY

But then, I prayed the right way for one month, five months, twelve months, two years . . . and God still kept me in a season of infertility. Suddenly, there was a battle I couldn't earn my way out of.

But then, I got up one morning and received a phone call that would rock my husband's and my life forever. We did all the right things, activating the prayer chain, crying out, speaking Scripture, believing big . . . and still, God let my husband's mom die. Suddenly, a battle without an end—a season I couldn't wish away.

And it was there—trapped on battlegrounds I never would have chosen for myself, empty to the point of exhaustion and completely unequipped, unprepared, and unarmed—where God met me. He peeled back layers of works-based religion, striving for acceptance, and prosperity gospel hopes to show me who He really is. He's the God who is in the battle, not above it. He's the God who walks with me in suffering, not who awaits me on the other side. He's the God who weaves victory in ways I could never have imagined, the one who allows the cusp of defeat to declare His power.

Are you on the battleground right now?

You're the girl who is embarrassed to ask for another prayer over anxiety because you thought you would have been strong enough to overcome it by now.

You're the girl held captive by an eating disorder, reciting over and over to yourself that your body is a temple but hating it all the same.

You're the girl who escaped home to come to college, wondering if your past will always define your present.

Or, you're the girl who's never seen a season of peace in the arms of Jesus; every single second has been a fight for as long as you can remember. The girl who's never read the Bible or has been mad at God for ages.

MOST HIGH

I believe that this week God wants to redefine the battle for us. He wants to give us a new and greater understanding of His victory. He wants to show us what it looks like to fight, what it looks like to win, and what *He* looks like in the midst of it. I even think that if we let Him, He can invite us to give our whole lives to Him through the Scripture we're about to read—for the very first time or in a fresh wave of surrender.

I'm ready if you are!

+ Turn in your Bible to 1 Samuel 17 and take a peek at the title. What story are we reading this week? Have you read or heard this story before? What do you remember about it?

Finally, we've made it to the most popular story in the books of 1 and 2 Samuel, and possibly one of the most popular stories in the whole Bible: *David and Goliath*. Guys, this tale is Sunday school royalty! So many of us, whether we were raised in Christian homes or not, grew up hearing the story of the little boy with a sling and some stones who slew a giant. And due to that popularity, you may be a little tempted to tune out this week because you've heard it all before. But I want to encourage you to lean in! We aren't just reading this story to learn it and be able to recite it to our children (though that's a fun perk). We get to read this moment in Scripture and encounter a living God. He can and will move and speak through His Word.

05 / GOD OF VICTORY

So let's take this chunk of Scripture step by step and see what God has to say. To start, read 1 Samuel 17:1–26.

+ Take some notes on what you read! What stood out to you from verses 1–26?

The Israelites, still under the leadership of King Saul, were set to face off against their OG enemy, the Philistines. The text paints a super vivid picture for us of the two armies camped across from each other with a valley of no-man's-land in between. Pacing around in that valley and swinging his sword is Goliath, the Philistine champion from the capital city of Gath. And apparently this dude is "six cubits and a span" in height. That's ancient Hebrew for *really, really tall* (likely over nine feet).

His role is pretty much to taunt the Israelites and make them scared. He offers a one-on-one battle that would determine the whole war. But clearly nobody likes the idea.

> *"On hearing the Philistine's words,*
> *Saul and all the Israelites were*
> *dismayed and terrified."*
> 1 Samuel 17:11

MOST HIGH

NOTES:

Then, verse 12 shifts the narrative to focus on the teenager we learned about last week named David. He's called onto the scene by his dad to deliver food to his brothers serving in the army. And little David doesn't like what he finds as Goliath does his intimidating spiel again.

"David asked the men standing near him, 'What will be done for the man who kills this Philistine and removes this disgrace from Israel? Who is this uncircumcised Philistine that he should defy the armies of the living God?'"
1 Samuel 17:26

It's almost as if the author is contrasting two points of view: Saul and his army versus David. And it's in that contrast that we can find our first point.

1. God is in the battle.

If we're looking closely, it's easy to tell who is handling the situation better. The well-trained, battle-ready men are running and hiding in fear every time Goliath shows up (verse 24) while the teenage shepherd boy with a Lunchable in hand is loudly declaring that this tall guy has nothing on the armies of the Most High (verse 26).

05 / GOD OF VICTORY

Do you wonder what the difference is? What could make people react so oppositely in the face of the same battle? Well, if we remember that God is the main character, it starts to become pretty clear. *They had different views about the God who put that battle in front of them.*

You see, David saw this whole thing for what it was: no threat to his God. It's like he put on sunglasses that shifted the view from man-vision to God-vision. David, empowered by the Spirit of God (remember what we read last week!) was able to see the obstacle ahead without fear because his courage was placed in Someone who had never failed, Someone who had promised to be with him, and Someone who had chosen Israel as His holy people. Goliath was only nine feet tall. And for David, God was so much bigger.

But Saul (who really should have been the champion willing to fight the giant) and his people were too caught up in how the circumstances appeared to fall back on what they knew about the God of victory. It's wild to think about because in the past few chapters of 1 Samuel, we see God win victory after victory for the Israelites. The only reason this battle suddenly seemed like too much and this giant suddenly seemed too big is because they had taken their eyes off the Lord.

Gosh, I'm convicted even just writing this! How many times have I allowed the circumstances in my life to cloud my view of the Lord? How many times have I stepped into battles terrified because I forgot that God was right there with me? How many Goliaths have I mistaken as taller than my Father in Heaven?

God's not asking us to venture onto any battlegrounds without Him. What if He wants to remind you that He is just as close in the hard times as in the easy times? I don't know about you, but if I have to fight either way, I'd much rather fight like David than cower like Saul.

MOST HIGH

+ What is your "battle" that can feel taller than God?

OK, I know you're itching to jump back into the story, so let's do it!

`Read 1 Samuel 17:27-40.`

David's older brother catches him strutting around the army camp talking a big game, and he takes the opportunity to try and knock little bro down a few pegs. Verses 28 and 29 take me back to sibling arguments in the back of my mom's minivan. Realistic, right? But apparently Eliab didn't shut his brother up well enough because eventually Saul hears what he's saying and summons David to his tent.

Fill in the blanks from `1 Samuel 17:32-33.`

"David said to Saul, 'Let no one lose heart on account of this Philistine; your servant will go and fight him.' Saul replied, 'You are _____ _____ to go out against this Philistine and fight him; you are only a _____ man, and he has been a warrior from his youth.'"

05 / GOD OF VICTORY

David wants to fight. Saul points out the obvious mismatch of skills, but God must see the whole thing a little differently.

2. God never needed you to be enough.

I'd bet that most of us have heard the same message that Saul tried to put David down with. *You're not able. You're too young. You're just you.*

+What do you hear said about you?

You're not able to _____ .
You're too _____ .
You're just _____ .

As weird as it is to consider it, Saul was technically correct here. David *was* unable to fight a seasoned, nine-foot-tall warrior. David *was* way too young to be talking such a big game in an army camp. And it could be the same for you! Maybe you are too young to be leading in the capacity you feel called to. Maybe you aren't able to quote the Scripture you think you should have memorized. Maybe you are just a freshman, just a sorority girl, or just a wallflower.

But there's something miraculous in David's answer that has the potential to change our perspectives permanently. He starts by telling Saul that he's got some credentials, fighting lions and bears and whatnot. But it's in verse 37 that the true power comes to light.

> *"'The LORD who rescued me from the paw of the lion and the paw of the bear will rescue me from the hand of this Philistine.'"*
> *1 Samuel 17:37a (emphasis added)*

David's power, equipping, and skillset didn't matter at all. It was God's power that counted. David was bold, but bold in God and not himself.[1] God never needed David to be enough because God was already enough for whatever battle He called David to face.

+ Find 2 Corinthians 12:9 and copy it down in the space below.

It's the best, most upside-down encouragement a girl can receive when facing the battle ahead of her: it's OK to be weak because God's power is made perfect in weakness.

I've seen this at play in my own life! When I step into a battleground season like the one I'm in right now, my instinct is always to try to "do it well." I want to be the best mourner, the best waiter, and the best sufferer there's ever been. But every single time, the longer the battle goes the less awesome I am at handling it. The pain forces me to my knees and brings me to a place where I'm barely getting out of bed, let alone setting some shining example of suffering in faith for the people around me. It's there, when I'm beaten down and on my knees, where I can humbly admit my weakness to God. It hits me . . . He wasn't waiting for me to be able to handle it on my own. He was simply waiting for me to fall back into His arms.

05 / GOD OF VICTORY

That's what we see in David's story! He tries to armor up, stepping into the impressive battle armor of a king. But then he realizes that he's not strong enough to carry the weight. So David steps into battle weak, defenseless, and only armed with what God has given him.

Somehow, weakness is the key to victory. *God never needed you to be enough because God is already enough for whatever battle He called you to face.*

Let's see how the story ends.

Read 1 Samuel 17:41-54.

3. God has the victory.

"David said to the Philistine, 'You come against me with sword and spear and javelin, but I come against you in the name of the LORD Almighty, the God of the armies of Israel, whom you have defied. This day the LORD will deliver you into my hands, and I'll strike you down and cut off your head. This very day I will give the carcasses of the Philistine army to the birds and the wild animals, and the whole world will know that there is a God in Israel. All those gathered here will know that it is not by sword or spear that the LORD saves; for the battle is the LORD's, and he will give all of you into our hands.'"
1 Samuel 17:45-47

MOST HIGH

+ Look at the verses on the page before and underline every time they mention God.

I think, cerebrally, most of us know that God is victorious. We've sung the songs over and over . . .

I'm gonna see a victory!
I'm gonna see a victory!
For the battle belongs to you Lord! [2]

But in our hearts we don't truly believe that victory or claim it for ourselves. We don't live like God won the battle for us. Honestly, most of the time we live like we're losers. Victims. If you feel that way today, my goal is to remind you of what Jesus won for you on the cross. God has the victory for your past, your present, and your eternity.

1 Corinthians 15:56 tells us that *the sting of death is sin*. It's an obvious truth when we look around! Our own sin poisons us, breaking our hearts, our souls, and our bodies down piece by piece. Our instinct has been to punch the kid who steals our toy since we were toddlers, and death has been ruling our lives from our first breath. No matter how many times we decide to "get our lives together" and try to abide by God's law, we inevitably fall short.

On our own, we're hopeless. But that's not how the story ends! 1 Corinthians 15:57 finishes the story:

> "But thanks be to God! He gives us the victory through our Lord Jesus Christ."

05 / GOD OF VICTORY

Jesus bridged the gap. Jesus saw us helpless, winless, and unequipped to fight against the torments of sin and death, so He stepped in. He lived a sinless, perfect life then died a torturous, criminal's death because He wanted to save *you*. He defeated the enemy—once and for all—tore the veil separating us from God, and rose again on the third day. He is still alive. He is still your advocate, seated at the right hand of the Father and standing with His hand out toward you.

His victory still stands.

This is an encouragement for all who would take His hand and give their whole life to Him. Even if you lose the battle in front of you here on earth, you have eternal victory in Heaven. But the eternal victory isn't all He did! Jesus's victory wasn't incomplete. Yes, He won tomorrow—but He also won *today*.

He won your fight with anxiety.

He won your fight with disordered eating.

He won your fight with your past, your lust, your loneliness, and your pride.

Jesus won! So can we live like it!?

As I was talking through this chapter with a friend, she said something profound: *walk like you've already won.*

THINK IT THROUGH!

+ Be honest . . . Have you ever given your life to Jesus and received His victory over the sin and death in your life? If yes, what was it like? If not, what do you think has been holding you back?

+ Take some time and dream with God. What would it look like for you to walk like you've already won in your current season? How would it be different from how you're walking now?

05 / GOD OF VICTORY

We are going to have to face battles. If you're in one right now, you know. And if you feel like you haven't hit the battle days yet, they're going to come. So get ready now! As Christians, covered by the victorious blood of Christ, we are called to step onto the battleground differently. It's a choice: do I walk like I'm victorious, or do I run in fear from the paths God is calling me to take?

I know, I know. It might feel kind of random to have a Jesus focus in a story about a little boy and a giant. But the whole Bible is about Jesus! This story screams His victory.

Both David and Jesus represented their people. Both David and Jesus fought battles on ground that rightfully belonged to God's people, ground they had lost. Both David and Jesus fought when their enemies were able to dominate the people of God through fear and intimidation alone. Both David and Jesus were sent to the battleground by their father. Both David and Jesus were scorned and rejected by the people who were supposed to be their family. Both David and Jesus fought their battles without concern for human strategies or conventional wisdom. Both David and Jesus fought a battle where victory was assured before they even started.[3]

If the Bible is Jesus's story, then the story of David and Goliath is ultimately pointing us toward Jesus and His victory. Jesus's victory is for *you*! Will you receive it? Whatever battleground you find yourself on today or in the future, look up to the Most High. Your God is bigger.

> "So David triumphed over the Philistine with a sling and a stone; without a sword in his hand he struck down the Philistine and killed him."
> 1 Samuel 17:50

CONVERSATION

1. Would you say you're in a battleground season right now? Why or why not?

2. Consider: Do you tend to view your battles more like Saul or like David? Why did you answer that way?

STARTERS

3. How does it make you feel to know that you're not enough, and God never needed you to be? Think back to the places where you fall short . . . How might God's power shine through in that area of weakness?

4. Have you ever given your life to Jesus and accepted His victory over your now and your forever? If so, what was it like? If not, what do you think has been holding you back?

GOD AND FRIENDSHIP

MOST HIGH

God and Friendship

> *Somehow, this is our last stop in 1 Samuel! Next week we'll jump into 2 Samuel (crazy, right!?). In this chapter, we're soaking up everything we can as we explore God's hand in the legendary friendship between David—the anointed one—and Jonathan—son of Saul.*

1 Samuel 18 – 23

Reading David's story in 1 and 2 Samuel is one of the most unique and robust theological pursuits in the whole Bible. Why? Because not only do we have a record of what he did (1 and 2 Samuel plus 1 and 2 Chronicles), but we also have behind-the-curtain access to how he *felt* and how he met with God in the midst of all that went on during his life and reign. His personal diary, songbook, and prayer book take up a large portion of the book of Psalms. And, even crazier, some of the psalms actually note which moments in his life spurred their authorship!

Psalm 54 is one of those gold-mine psalms. Take a few minutes to read through it as we center our hearts for this week's study. It's clearly a cry for help in a hard moment for David. *Save me, God,* he writes. *Hear my prayer.* Can you think of a time when you begged God to save you? When you beg God to hear you and to save you, your heart is on its last breath. You're *desperate*.

06 / GOD AND FRIENDSHIP

And that's where David was at as he penned Psalm 54. And check out the little headline in your Bible: *When the Ziphites had gone to Saul and said, "Is David not hiding among us?"* This is part of the story we are studying in this chapter! We have direct access to David's feelings while he was going through what we're about to study this week! How cool is that!?

> *Flip to 1 Samuel 23 and read verses 14-19.*

Now, we'll get into the nitty gritty details later in this chapter, but this moment in Scripture records David hiding out in the wilderness because Saul was intent on killing him. It goes as far as to say that Saul sought him *every day.* His panic and desperation make a lot of sense! I think I'd be freaking out too if someone was actively trying to murder me and I was hiding near some snitches (e.g., the Ziphites).

But the murder and the snitches aren't what we're going to focus on this week. God wasn't worried about those guys. In the midst of a hard moment, God dropped a beautiful gift in David's lap. Can you guess what it was?

NOTES:

MOST HIGH

+ Look back at 1 Samuel 23:14–19. What's the gift God gave David in his hard moment?

With his life on the line, God brought David just what he needed: a *friend*.

This week we're going to trace the timeline of one of the most famous friendships in the Bible: David and Jonathan. Somehow, in the midst of the messiest, grittiest, and most drama-filled story, God allowed a beautiful friendship to blossom.

Against all odds, David and Jonathan's friendship remains a picture of God's heart for holy friendships and relationships.

Now, the Psalm 54 moment between David and Jonathan was actually the end of their story together, so let's go back in time and start at the beginning —when David and Jonathan met for the very first time—and see what God has in store for us.

Read 1 Samuel 18:1-5

1. *God calls us to love.*

06 / GOD AND FRIENDSHIP

Have you ever met someone you instantly clicked with? It happened to me once at a high school choir camp. I met this girl named Tasha, and after one conversation we declared we were soul sisters and spent the rest of the camp attached at the hip. All the other campers thought we had known each other for years, and honestly it felt like we had. I imagine that's how it felt for David and Jonathan. One joke from David or one playful shove from Jonathan, and boom—they were besties.

> *"After David had finished talking with Saul, Jonathan became one in spirit with David, and he loved him as himself."*
> 1 Samuel 18:1

This moment comes right after David defeated Goliath (like, *right after*). Conceivably, David's still holding Goliath's severed head (yup, that's gross). Saul decided to keep David close by, meaning an end to his shepherding era and close quarters with Saul's favorite son (and the clear successor to Saul's throne): Jonathan. There's this beautiful moment where Jonathan gives David all of his stuff and, right there on the battleground, they make a covenant with each other to be BFFs forever. (If it sounds dramatic, think back to your fourth-grade bestie you had matching necklaces with. We've got no room to judge.)

The wording in verse 1 might ring a few bells for you if you've spent time in the Word.

MOST HIGH

+ Find Leviticus 19:18 and copy it down in the space below.

+ Now do the same for Matthew 22:39.

God has consistently shown us all throughout Scripture that we are called to love our neighbors as ourselves. It can't be a coincidence that Jonathan and David shared that sentiment at the beginning of their friendship. It's an obvious guide for us. (Gosh, I love it when God makes things obvious!) The starting point to a godly friendship is to love our friends the way God calls us to love.

Jonathan takes it even further as we keep reading. Did you catch the symbolism of his actions as he hands over his robe? Remember, Jonathan should have been next in line for the throne!

06 / GOD AND FRIENDSHIP

So he's making more than just a personal statement to David, but a *political* one. He's symbolically giving David the position of Saul's successor, forfeiting his right as heir.[1] This is crazy if you really think about it, and it's so clearly the hand of God. Jonathan sets aside his own ambitions and birthright to yield to the one God has chosen.

That's crazy, sacrificial love. It's love that's deeper than surface-level, convenient friendship. It's choosing to love when it's *inconvenient*. It's love that crosses boundary lines and puts the other person in front of oneself.

That kind of love reminds me of *Jesus*, the best example of love.

> *"Very rarely will anyone die for a righteous person, though for a good person someone might possibly dare to die. But God demonstrates his own love for us in this: While we were still sinners, Christ died for us."*
> Romans 5:7–8

Jesus set the ultimate standard for what it means to love our friends (and even our enemies). Doesn't that make you want to activate that same love in your own friendships? I want to be the friend who puts my friend's needs above my own. I want to be the friend who steps behind my friend and lets her take the spotlight. I want to be the friend who loves my friend *as I love myself* and, even more importantly, *as Jesus loves me*.

MOST HIGH

+ Can you think of a time when someone loved you like Jesus? What was it like? How did it make you feel?

Jonathan and David's friendship began on the right foot, with deep roots of commitment and a heart to love each other as God calls us to love. But it wasn't all sunshine and roses ahead. Jonathan was still the son of a crazy king who had stepped out of God's favor. And David had just become public enemy number one.

After David killed Goliath, he became popular with the people of Israel. So popular, in fact, that the people were comparing him to Saul. *Saul has slain his thousands,* they sang. But *David his tens of thousands* (1 Samuel 18:7). Obviously, Saul didn't like that. He resolved to keep a close eye on David from that point on. His jealousy grew by the day, leading him to frequently try to murder David out of fear that he would take the kingdom out from under him.

That's where we pick up as we continue reading a few chapters later. Read 1 Samuel chapter 20. (While you're reading, pay special attention to the way David and Jonathan interact with each other.)

Take notes from your reading on the next page!

06 / GOD AND FRIENDSHIP

NOTES:

After narrowly escaping an assassination attempt thanks to Saul's daughter Michal, David is fed up. He meets with Jonathan to see if his friend has turned on him like it seems everyone else had. Jonathan answers with the godly love we've come to expect from him.

Fill in the blanks from 1 Samuel 20:17.

"And Jonathan had David reaffirm his oath out of _____ for him, because he _____ him as he _____ himself."

Together, they cooked up a plan to test Saul's heart and see if he really was intent on killing David. You see, sweet Jonathan had trouble believing the worst of his father. David, on the other hand, had one too many spears thrown at him to be as optimistic as his friend. It's there, in the tensest of moments, that we see another piece to the puzzle of God's heart for friendship: we commit, even when it's hard.

2. God calls us to invest in friendship—even when it's hard.

Amber is one of my oldest and closest friends. We survived high school, college, and post-grad together. We led Delight side by side, she was a bridesmaid in my wedding, and I was a bridesmaid in hers. But there was a period of about a year in the middle of all that when we didn't talk to each other at all.

MOST HIGH

To give you some context, I suffered from a chronic illness that spanned my late high school years and early college, exactly the years when my relationship with Amber blossomed. But then, my sophomore year of college, God miraculously healed me out of the blue. (I'm not kidding! It was wild!) And it took me a while to adjust to a new, healthy normal. I was finding out who I was apart from my illness and also doing that normal character growth that happens in college. You're not the same gal you were in high school, right?

But the issue was that I felt like Amber wasn't letting me grow. It seemed like she talked to me like I was still sick when I was healed. She treated me like the high school me when college me was, in my opinion, much better. I felt tied down, held back, and honestly a little talked down to. So I did what anybody would do.

I ghosted her for a year.

OK, please don't judge me! I'm trying to be vulnerable here. Hindsight is twenty-twenty. Obviously, looking back, I'm aware that I handled it wrong. When the friendship was easy and made me feel good, I stayed and poured into it. But the second it took work, the second it felt hard, and the second it wasn't serving me, I jumped ship. I left her stranded without an explanation for a whole year, just because I was too afraid to have a hard conversation with her and because I wasn't committed to investing in the loving relationship God had planted me in.

When we finally had that hard convo a year too late, I'll never forget what she said. *I'm so sorry I made you feel that way. I want to be a better friend to you!* I shouldn't have been surprised; she'd always been quick to apologize when she'd messed up. But it was her next statement that settled deep in my heart: *I wish you had just told me.*

Jonathan was willing to put his life on the line and betray his family for his friend, but I wasn't willing to have one honest conversation for

06 / GOD AND FRIENDSHIP

mine. If you're real with yourself, are you the same way? Think of that friendship that came on fast then fizzled out. Think of that friend who hurt you so you dropped her. Think of the girl who an acquaintance said was "toxic" so you blacklisted her. Ladies, this is not God's design! God calls us to invest in godly friendships even when they're hard!

Fill in the blanks from 1 Corinthians 13:4-7.

"Love is patient, love is kind. It does not envy, it does not boast, it is not proud. It does not _____ others, it is not self-seeking, it is not easily angered, it keeps __ _____ of wrongs. Love does not delight in evil but rejoices with the truth. It always protects, always trusts, always hopes, always _____."

If God called you to love your friends, He's also calling you to *keep* loving them when it's hard. Now, I'm not talking about staying in an abusive relationship or allowing a toxic friendship to lead you away from God! Of course we need to use discernment about which relationships God is calling us to invest in. But for those good, God-ordained friendships . . . He says they're worth fighting for like Jonathan fought for David.

NOTES:
_____
_____
_____
_____
_____
_____

THINK IT THROUGH!

+ **Can you think of a time you didn't invest in a friendship when you should have? What was it like?**

+ **Consider the current relationships in your life. Which do you feel called to invest in?**

06 / GOD AND FRIENDSHIP

Alright, we've finally made it back to where we started: the end.

+ Copy 1 Samuel 23:16 in the space below.

[ ]

Here we are again in Jonathan and David's last moments together. Spoiler alert: David will continue to be on the run for years after this moment, and Jonathan will eventually die with his father, Saul, at the end of 1 Samuel. In one of David's lowest moments (the moment that prompted him to write Psalm 54), Jonathan offered him encouragement, reaffirming his calling and the covenant they had made with each other. But it's verse 16 that I want us to land on for this week. Go back to what you wrote in the box above and circle, "helped him find strength in God."

3. God calls us to help our friends find strength in Him.

We were never made to do life alone. In our hardest moments, God gives us the people around us to strengthen us, to encourage us, and to point us in the right direction. And He gives us to others to do the same. But there's something crucial here that we can't forget as we follow God's design for friendship: *our friendships aren't about us—they're about Him!*

MOST HIGH

How would your friendships change if God was the main character in them? Jonathan could have tried to hype David up on his own, giving him surface-level compliments and telling him he's got this. But instead the Word of God remembers him as someone who helped his friend find strength *in God*, not in himself.

We are called to be friends who are quick to pray for each other, not quick to spout out the first advice that comes to our heads.

We are called to be friends who speak life over each other and point each other to the Word, not friends who offer surface-level encouragement.

We are called to be friends who call each other out and call each other higher in love, not friends who just pretend like everything's OK.

It's such a helpful tool for determining the health of your relationships! The healthiest way to love others, to invest in them, and to strengthen them is to acknowledge that God first loved you, invested in you, and strengthened you. It's through Him that you even have the ability to be a friend at all, let alone to do it well.

Sheesh! This Scripture is calling us to do some soul-searching. Am I putting God first in my friendships? Am I truly loving the way He's called me to love? Do I even have any friendships that match His design?

+ Take some time to process the questions above . . . How might God be challenging you in your relationships through this Scripture?

06 / GOD AND FRIENDSHIP

Isn't it crazy that a turbulent friendship between two dudes who lived thousands of years ago can speak directly into our lives today as college women trying to navigate community, roommates, and dating? God's Word is pretty cool like that! But where does this all leave us? What do we do now?

Some of us will read about David and Jonathan and feel empowered. We know exactly which friends we can pour into even better, and we're excited to watch those relationships thrive.

Others of us will read about God's design for friendship and Jonathan's love and loyalty and feel conviction. We know we haven't been that kind of friend in a long time. We step away from this asking God to make us better and to draw us closer to His heart.

But I know there are a lot of us reading this who could leave feeling discouraged because we just don't have any of the friends we desperately desire to have. Trust me; I've been in your shoes! College is hard enough, and watching everyone around you seemingly find besties immediately while you feel left out and left behind doesn't make it any easier. So I want to speak to you as we close this out.

Sister, there is hope for you. God loves you just as much as he loved David and just as much as he loved Jonathan. Community is and has always been His design. He was anti-loneliness all the way back in the Garden of Eden. He desires and plans to bring you the life-giving friendships you dream of, even if the journey there looks different from the people around you.

I want to encourage you to lean into your Delight community and try out the boldness to ask a girl out to coffee or to spark up a conversation with the girl sitting next to you in class. But, most of all, keep your eyes focused on God, the very best friend. He can be enough for you even before He brings you the people He's promised.

We love because He first loved us. What a miracle! *God, we're after your heart!*

CONVERSATION

1. Heart Check: How good of a friend are you?

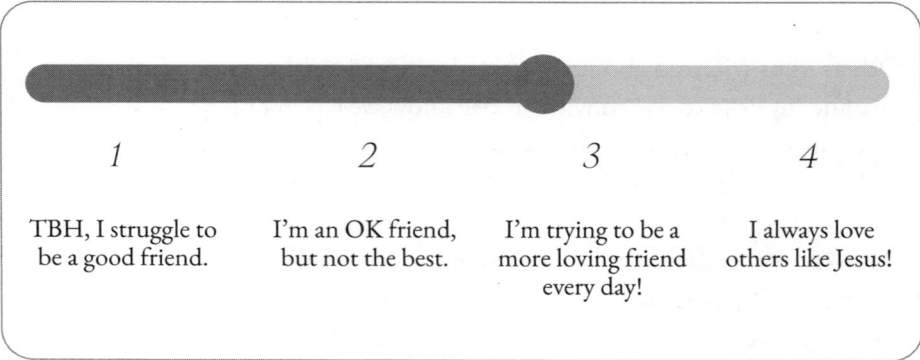

1	2	3	4
TBH, I struggle to be a good friend.	I'm an OK friend, but not the best.	I'm trying to be a more loving friend every day!	I always love others like Jesus!

2. Do you have a friendship that's extra hard right now? How might God be calling you to invest in that friendship in this season?

STARTERS

3. Can you think of a time when a friend strengthened you in the Lord like Jonathan did for David? What was it like? (If not, we encourage you to spend some time in prayer asking the Lord to bring you a friend like Jonathan!)

4. Jesus is the best friend to us! How has He been a good friend to you?

HOLY GOD

MOST HIGH

Holy God

> We've finally made it to 2 Samuel! Thank you, God, for such an amazing adventure through Your Word! This week we're exploring the holiness of God and learning what it means for us today.

1 Samuel 4:1 – 11 & 2 Samuel 6:1 – 15

I learned about God's holiness in elementary school, the first time I was allowed to be an acolyte—the one who was in charge of lighting the candles—at my grandparents' Lutheran church on a Sunday morning. I remember softly sneaking down the aisle while everyone was shaking hands and exchanging pleasantries. I slipped into the little closet at the corner of the sanctuary and carefully put on the child-size white robe that hung on a hook. I tied a white rope around my waist and grabbed the long, golden candlestick.

I held my breath as I tried to gracefully walk down the aisle, so aware that everyone was watching each step I took with the small flame held out in front of me. I remember my little feet stopping right before I stepped onto the altar, bowing before I walked onto what felt like sacred ground. Then, slowly, I lit each candle that sat around the beautiful altar with the huge wooden cross and the stained glass window. With a smile from the pastor —my job done—I hopped off to sit in the special seat for the acolytes.

At that age, I hadn't read the Bible cover to cover yet. I couldn't quote the gospel story by memory. But I had notebooks filled with a little girl's prayers for every person I knew.

07 / HOLY GOD

I had my very own Bible with the first two chapters of Genesis highlighted completely in neon green. That little girl had even heard God speak to her in a dream, my favorite memory with the Lord still to this day.

I think the childlike faith of a kid who still couldn't do multiplication paved the way for an awe and reverence for God that easily gets forgotten in today's day and age. I knew how much of a privilege it was to wear the white robe, even if I didn't understand the symbolism behind it. I felt the reverence of the altar, bowing in God's presence before I had read Bible stories about ancient men who had done the same. My eyes were wide in wonder, so sure that God was watching my every move as those candles were lit one by one.

He was so *holy* and I could feel Him smiling down at me.

Here are my questions for us this week as we explore Scripture: Do you see God as holy? Do you *treat* God as holy? My guess is that for most of us—myself included—the answer would be no. Sure, we respect Him and we know He's our King, but we're not often led to marvel at His holiness or to truly understand what His holiness even means.

Luckily, the stories we're reading in this chapter scream God's holiness loud and clear. Why? Because they're all about *the Ark of the Covenant.*

+ Real quick, before we dive into our reading, list what you already know about the Ark of the Covenant below. Have you heard of it before? What do you remember about it, if anything?

MOST HIGH

There are probably thousands of books and podcasts and movies and sermons about the Ark of the Covenant. It's a popular pathway of study for theologians, mostly because of its rich history, the symbolism it holds for both the Jewish and Christian faiths, and because nobody knows where it is now (we love a good mystery!). We can't get into everything for the sake of this study, so let me give us a lightning-fast review so we feel armed with some context for the conversation ahead.

Fun Facts About the Ark of the Covenant!

- The Ark of the Covenant is first mentioned in Exodus, where it is presented as the location from which Yahweh (God) promises to speak to Moses as a king speaks to his advisor from a throne.[1] Essentially, it's a physical representation of God's presence on earth!

-Inside the Ark at one point was a jar of manna (the food God gave the Israelites when they were wandering the wilderness), Aaron's staff (Moses's brother and a priest), and the tablets containing the Ten Commandments.

-There are a *lot* of regulations and rules in Scripture for how to handle the Ark (check out Leviticus 16 if you're curious).

-The Ark's design is described in crazy specific detail in the Bible. Here's what it probably looked like:

07 / HOLY GOD

Guys, studying the Ark is such a rabbit hole! We could spend weeks on this! So let's just go ahead and dive into the Word.

> Read 1 Samuel 4:1-11.

1. We can't use God.

We've gone back in time a little bit from where we ended up last week. This story takes place pre-David *and* pre-Saul. It actually occurs when Eli, Samuel's mentor, is still the top dog in Israel. And, as is usually the case when it comes to ancient Israel, they were at war with the Philistines. But this time, they were defeated.

> *"When the soldiers returned to camp, the elders of Israel asked, 'Why did the L*ORD *bring defeat on us today before the Philistines? Let us bring the ark of the* L*ORD'S covenant from Shiloh, so that he may go with us and save us from the hand of our enemies.'"*
> 1 Samuel 4:3

At first glance, this might seem like the right move. They lost the first battle, so why not bring God into it to win the second battle? But there are two pretty glaring things wrong with their thought process.

MOST HIGH

First of all, the Ark isn't God. They decided to bring this golden box with them so that God would go with them, like God was inside the box ready to be carted around at will. But we know that's not how God rolls. It sounds to me like the Israelites had been influenced by the idol-worshiping cultures all around them. Somehow, the Ark had changed from a reminder of God's glory and a holy meeting place to a man-made container of an actual god. This is definitely bad territory for their minds to wander into.

But there's something even deeper happening here. You see, this "trick" had worked for them before. Back in the book of Joshua, God told them to bring the Ark as they marched around the walls of Jericho (Joshua 6:6). And in an epic battle against the Midianites that God charged Moses to undertake, they carried all the temple artifacts (Numbers 31:6). It makes sense, right? It worked before! Why wouldn't it work again?

But here's the difference: this time, they didn't seek God for direction. It wasn't Him who told them to march into the battle with the Ark. The Israelites remembered what God's power could do, so they tried to use that power for themselves without submitting to His will. They heard secondhand what God was capable of and tried to reap the blessings without entering into a relationship with the blesser.

07 / HOLY GOD

Essentially, *they used a God they weren't willing to obey*. And, obviously, things turned out badly.

Now, this might seem like one of those stories that is cool to read about but has zero applicability to our modern, college-girl lives. But I want to challenge you to look deeper. I think there's almost nothing more relevant for this day and age than this.

Take manifestation for example. It's the trending belief that you can speak what you want from the world into existence. We're manifesting good grades, cute boyfriends, and nice weather. And, on the surface, you could back this up with Scripture. Proverbs 21 says that our words have the power of life and death, right? You could argue that manifesting is just harnessing that power.

But isn't that just the same as what the Israelites tried to do with the Ark? We hear that God has the power to do something, so we try to take that power for ourselves. Without seeking His will, His presence, or His heart, we try to steal the benefits of His power. Instead of speaking His Word or declaring His truth, we decide to speak our own words and declare our own truths.

We're using God. We do it when we swear on His name in casual conversation, when we say that He told us to do something when we know He didn't, and when the only times we come to Him in prayer are when we need something from Him. We do it when we twist Scripture to fit our needs and when we only claim to be a Christian when it's convenient.

Gosh, it can be a hard pill to swallow, but this is such a crucial truth! *If your God is just a genie in a bottle, you're headed toward death and defeat.*

MOST HIGH

+ **Can you think of a time when you "used" God? Get super real and honest about it in the space below.**

So, the Israelites tried to use God's power without His presence, and they were defeated. The Ark got carried away by the enemy, some plagues happened (check out 1 Samuel 5 if you're curious), and it ended up in Kiriath-Jearim, a city northwest of Jerusalem. There it sat for twenty years.

It doesn't end there, though! The story picks back up in 2 Samuel. Go ahead and read 2 Samuel 6:1–11.

Remember where we left off last week. David was on the run and Saul was in his crazy era. Well, between then and where we pick up now in 2 Samuel 6, *a lot* went down. (Please read through the chapters we skipped in your free time! I promise it's worth it!) Essentially, Saul and Jonathan died in battle, David formed a Robin-Hood-like war band and fought lots of battles, and—eventually—David became king of Israel. His first act as king of a unified Israel was to secure Jerusalem as his ruling city and to defeat the Philistines in battle.

But David knew his holy city was missing something, so he started an expedition to bring the Ark of God's presence home. But, as we read, things didn't go as planned. Turns out, God isn't someone to mess with.

07 / HOLY GOD

2. Fear of the Lord is a good thing.

I read a quote in a book once that stuck with me so much that I wrote it on a sticky note and kept it on my desk for years. Dallas Willard wrote that *God is not mean, but He is dangerous.*[2] This story in 2 Samuel obviously illustrates that idea. It's almost a jump scare! There they are, moving the Ark, then *bam*, someone gets struck down.

> *"When they came to the threshing floor of Nakon, Uzzah reached out and took hold of the ark of God, because the oxen stumbled. The Lord's anger burned against Uzzah because of his irreverent act; therefore God struck him down, and he died there beside the ark of God."*
> 2 Samuel 6:6-7

I don't know about you, but I was kind of confused and uncomfortable when I first read this story. Poor Uzzah! What about God's kindness and grace? Did he really deserve to die?

Before we get too deep into this, let me tell you that it's OK to ask questions of the text when you're reading the Bible. God isn't afraid of your questions, He's not afraid of your doubts, and His understanding has no limit (Psalm 147:5). Translation: He gets it! He knows that all the smiting that goes down in the Old Testament is hard to swallow. So lean in and let Him speak to you through the Word as you seek to understand.

MOST HIGH

To really understand Uzzah's death, we have to zoom out a little bit and check out the events surrounding it. David's heart was in the right place to desire to bring the Ark home, but as we look closely, we see he went about it in the wrong way.

First, they put the Ark on a cart (verse 3). God specifically told the Isrealites in Numbers 4:15 that the holy things had to be carried by priests, not on a wagon. *Strike one.* Then, it was David and his men who surrounded the cart on the walk because that was what "seemed right to all the people" (1 Chronicles 13:4). But God had clearly said the Ark was only to be carried by Levites. *Strike two.* The whole thing had turned into a parade when it was supposed to be an act of worship. And then, Uzzah reached out to touch the Ark. Numbers 4:15 again warns that they "must not touch the holy things or they will die." *Strike three.*

The expedition was doomed from the start, and Uzzah's death was the unfortunate consequence of the casual way they handled God's Ark.

Fill in the blank from 2 Samuel 6:9-10.

"David was _____ of the Lord that day and said, 'How can the ark of the Lord ever come to me?' He was not willing to take the ark of the Lord to be with him in the City of David. Instead, he took it to the house of Obed-Edom the Gittite."

Fear of the Lord and reverence toward God are almost obsolete conversations these days. We tend to serve a casual God who's chill and laid-back. But when we read stories like these, that casual-God theory flies right out the window. Does the God of 2 Samuel seem chill to you? No way! And sister, He was the same God then as He is now. *He's not mean, but He is dangerous.*

07 / HOLY GOD

As Christians, we are called to have a healthy fear of the Lord. This doesn't mean that we're supposed to walk around terrified that God's going to strike us down when we make a mistake. But it means that we have a holistic understanding of His holiness and a proper reverence for Him as our King and our Creator. We trust His grace-filled heart as our Father, but we also bow to His leadership.

A healthy fear of the Lord should change the way we act.

Think about David and his buddies in this story! They didn't show a fear of the Lord when they partied along the way with the Ark, and the consequences were severe—so much so that David left the Ark there without finishing the job (verse 11). Their lack of reverence caused a casual attitude toward their King.

It's the same for us! When we put God in a little box and make Him a side character in our lives, we're walking on shaky ground. It's like putting a bomb in your backpack and walking around town. You're playing with fire!

But when we remember the gravity of our God, the power and majesty of the Creator of the Universe, a holy fear fills our hearts. Suddenly, He's the main character of our story. We begin to seek His heart for decisions before we make them, we start to pore over the Scriptures because we want to live our lives the way He designed, and we stop talking lightly about Him. We begin to take sin seriously, and we repent often. We enter into moments of worship with a new depth because we are more aware of who it is that we're worshiping and how worth the worship He really is.

Fear of the Lord is a good thing because it makes us walk in alignment with Him. And trust me, walking His way is much better than the alternative.

THINK IT THROUGH!

+ Do you think you have a healthy fear of the Lord? Why or why not?

+ As we discussed on the page before, reverence for God leads us to ask God for guidance, stirs up obedience, encourages us to take His name seriously, leads us to repentance when we sin, and deepens our worship. Which of these do you most want to grow in? Why?

07 / HOLY GOD

OK, I'm ready to move on from the smiting. Luckily, this story has a happy ending! Read 2 Samuel 6:12–15.

As the Ark sat where David had left it in the house of Obed-Edom for three months, God blessed Obed and his entire household. And that blessing from the hand of God was just what David needed to return to his senses. It was a reminder to him that it is more natural and in character for God to bless than to curse. So David consulted the rules God had given them for the transport of His Ark, and he moved it the right way: right into Jerusalem.

> *"Wearing a linen ephod, David was dancing before the Lord with all his might, while he and all Israel were bringing up the ark of the Lord with shouts and the sound of trumpets."*
> *2 Samuel 6:14-15*

It's a beautiful picture of redemption and an accurate placement of honor. They revered the Lord, chose to obey His commands out of a holy fear, and they *danced* with joy. The presence of God was returned home, finally!

It's an awesome story, but thousands of years separate us from these events. And something huge has changed since then thanks to one man: *Jesus.*

3. *God is still holy.*

God is still the same today as He was then. He is just as holy. He is just as awe-inspiring. He is just as dangerous. But what's changed? Why are we able to get close to Him, to be adopted as His children, and approach Him in intimate relationship when David, a man after God's own heart, had to jump through hoops just to be safe in His presence?

MOST HIGH

The answer lies in the gospel story.

Fill in the blank from Matthew 27:51a.
"At that moment the curtain of the temple was _____ in _____ from top to bottom"

At the cross, as Jesus took His last breath, the temple curtain separating the inner, most holy place and the outer, more accessible place was torn in two. Symbolic? Yes! But there's more to it than that! When Jesus defeated sin and death on our behalf, He created a new pathway for unity with God. He gave us His righteousness so that we could stand before God clean and pure. Thanks to Jesus, we don't have to jump through hoops to get near God's presence. Thanks to Jesus and the movement of the Holy Spirit, the presence of God is just a breath away for those who believe!

> *"Let us then approach God's throne of grace with confidence, so that we may receive mercy and find grace to help us in our time of need."*
> Hebrews 4:16

Y'all, this is crazy! The Israelites would have *killed* to have the access to God that we have now on the other side of the resurrection. Ancient Jews wouldn't even say the name of God out loud out of fear of His power, and somehow we're invited to approach God's holy presence with confidence—the same presence that used to blind those who even looked upon it. Every single time we seek God in prayer, every time we repent and receive forgiveness, and every time we worship is a miraculous encounter with a holy God!

He is still holy! He is still so much more, so much better, and so much grander than we could ever wrap our minds around! *But do we treat Him as such?*

07 / HOLY GOD

What a waste it is to have the one who created the universe in our grasp and only look to Him when we need something. We have an all-powerful Father, and we use Him for party tricks. Jesus Christ died for the access to God we now have, and we go weeks forgetting to even pray. Let this be your wake-up call! The invitation is there for all who would receive it: encounter a holy God today!

Try getting on your knees and taking off your shoes in His presence next time you pray. Do you feel the difference?

Try starting with awe, wonder, and gratitude before you ask Him for something. Do you feel the difference?

Try approaching His Word with a holy reverence, working out your salvation with fear and trembling (Philippians 2:12). Do you feel the difference?

We have the honor and the privilege of serving—not using—a holy God who is worth every bit of our reverence. It's a new heart posture—one that prepares you for forever.

Because God was holy then, He's holy now, and He will be holy in Heaven when we see Him face-to-face.

> *"Day and night they never stop saying: "Holy, holy, holy is the LORD God Almighty," who was, and is, and is to come."'*
> *Revelation 4:8b–c*

CONVERSATION

1. What stood out to you the most from this week's chapter and Scripture? How did this lesson change or deepen your perception of God, if at all?

2. We discussed manifestation as one way that we try to use God. Consider: What other ways can we be tempted to use God? Which ways do you find showing up most in your own life?

STARTERS

3. On a scale from one to ten, how would you rate your level of healthy fear of the Lord (ten being the most, one being the least)? Why did you answer that way?

4. Look back at the second *"Think it through"* question on page 144. Which option did you choose? What tangible steps can you take this week to grow in that area?

GOD, WORTHY OF WORSHIP

MOST HIGH

God, Worthy of Worship

> *I think God wants to give us a worship refresh this week as we continue on in 2 Samuel. Whatever your life looks like right now, allow Him to blow a fresh wind into your heart as you open up His Word.*

2 Samuel 6:16 – 7:29

OK, brace yourself, because I feel the need to get a little vulnerable here.

I've always been too much. Now, I don't say this in a "pick me" way where I need you to tell me I'm not too much, because I'm actually very aware that I am. I got kicked out of the church choir in third grade for singing too loud. In sixth grade, my teacher showed a video of me dancing to all of her classes because she thought it was so funny and over the top (admittedly, I got wayyyy too into the step touch). Even just yesterday, someone asked me to "do a little less" while I was helping lead worship at church.

Too much, too big, too loud, too weird, too extra . . . It's the story of my life! And it took me a lot of years and a lot of prayers and a lot of tears to get to the point where I knew that God didn't see me as "too much." I now happily put the blame on Him. He made me this way, so He must like me this way!

And I can't help but wonder if David ever felt like too much. We read about his anointing story when he wasn't even invited to the party, and I wonder if it's because he tended to be a little obnoxious at dinner.

08 / GOD, WORTHY OF WORSHIP

We see his big mouth getting him into trouble in the story of David and Goliath, and I wonder if he felt embarrassed about it as he lay in bed that night. And the story we're learning from today really is the nail in the coffin. If "too much" had a poster child, it was King David.

Read 2 Samuel 6:16-23.

This week we're adoring and exploring a God who is worth our worship, a God who is so beautiful and so praiseworthy that the only appropriate response is a life sold-out and on-fire for him. Are you undignified and completely abandoned for Jesus? Let this Scripture challenge you to be a little more "too much" for the glory of God.

1. *Your worship is for God.*

This portion of 2 Samuel picks up right after what we read last week about the return of the Ark of the Covenant to Israel. David had finally done things God's way and was praising his heart out as they entered into the holy city. The text says that he was "dancing before the Lord with all his might" (2 Samuel 6:14), so I'm picturing some wild moves. But there was one person who didn't like his display of worship.

> "As the ark of the Lord was entering the City of David, Michal daughter of Saul watched from a window. And when she saw King David leaping and dancing before the Lord, she despised him in her heart."
> 2 Samuel 6:16

MOST HIGH

David's wife, Michal, definitely did not approve of the way David was conducting himself. In her mind, a king should have acted with more decorum. She even went as far as to tell him that he was being *vulgar* since he had traded his kingly robes for a priestly garment called an ephod. Translation: in Michal's eyes, David was "too much."

But David's response rocks my world every single time I read it.

Fill in the blanks from 2 Samuel 6:21-22.

*"David said to Michal, 'It was before the _____, who chose me rather than your father or anyone from his house when he appointed me ruler over the L*ORD*'s people Israel—I will celebrate before the ___. I will become even more _____ than this, and I will be humiliated in my own eyes. But by these slave girls you spoke of, I will be held in honor.'"*

David's answer is simple: *I did it for God, not for you.*

What would you do if Jesus walked into the room you're in right now? You're in your dorm and Jesus opens the door and walks in. You're at a coffee shop and Jesus pulls out the chair next to you. You're sitting in the hall outside your next class and you see Jesus walking toward you.

Think about it! How would you react?

I bet some of us would sit up a little straighter and fix our hair. Some of us would immediately start crying, some of us would drop to our knees, and others of us would sprint up to Him for a hug. I would probably do

08 / GOD, WORTHY OF WORSHIP

something massively embarrassing like break out into my own rendition of "Oceans" by Hillsong.

That automatic response to the presence of God is built into us, triggered when His Holy Spirit is allowed the space to move freely. For David, his praise bubbled up so fiercely that all he could do was dance. And it may be the same for you or something completely different. This worship response built into us isn't a one-size-fits-all situation! One person's "too much" may be another person's "just right"! But there's one common denominator: Jesus is the one you're focusing on.

If David had his eyes set on anyone other than the Lord, he probably would have noticed Michal's judgemental stare and started to tone things down. Instead of "undignified" worship, the Bible would have memorialized this moment as "half-hearted" worship. It's the same for us in our worship moments and in our day-to-day lives!

You sing a little too loud in worship at church and notice the person next to you glance over. Immediately, you lower your volume.

You tell your friends about a crazy encounter you had with the Lord in your prayer time that morning, but when you see their doubtful faces, you start to question if it really happened the way you remember.

You strike up a conversation with a stranger, excited to have the chance to share the gospel. But once they share that they have had bad experiences with Christians, you steer the conversation to "safer" topics.

We're called to live, act, sing, and worship like the King is in the room. And the only way to do that is to tear your eyes away from the people around you and turn them back to the all-consuming, beautiful presence of Jesus. And the miracle is that our pure response to His presence is never too much for Him. *He loves when you love Him with all you've got!*

MOST HIGH

+ Can you think of the time when a "Michal" got in the way of you authentically responding to the presence of Jesus? Describe the situation below.

```
┌─────────────────────────────────────────────────┐
│                                                 │
│                                                 │
│                                                 │
│                                                 │
└─────────────────────────────────────────────────┘
```

Let's keep moving in the text. Now, the Ark has been returned and David has settled into life as King in Jerusalem. And in just a few seemingly insignificant verses, I believe God has hidden a lifetime of lessons for us. Check it out:

> *"After the king was settled in his palace and the Lord had given him rest from all his enemies around him, he said to Nathan the prophet, 'Here I am, living in a house of cedar, while the ark of God remains in a tent.' Nathan replied to the king, 'Whatever you have in mind, go ahead and do it, for the Lord is with you.'"*
> *2 Samuel 7:1–3*

2. Your whole life can be worship.

08 / GOD, WORTHY OF WORSHIP

As David got cozy in his fancy palace, his heart still didn't feel at rest. He noticed that while he lived in glamor and splendor, the Ark (a representation of God's presence) was sitting in a tent. In that moment, a dream ignited in David's heart to build a permanent home for God's presence, a temple that would rival the beauty of anything ever constructed thus far in history. He wanted to give God more glory, more honor, and more praise.

Even David's dreams were to worship the Lord!

We'll get deeper into the temple background as we continue on in the text, but we've gotta stop here and dig our heels in. The authentic praise we saw bubbling up from David as he danced for God in chapter 6 didn't stop in that moment of public, corporate worship. That same praise for God flowed into his *life,* his everyday moments, goals, thoughts, and decisions.

Think about it. How would our lives look different if we treated every moment as an opportunity for worship? I'm going to sound like a broken record here, but it all comes back to who the main character of your story is. I'd venture to say that if God is the main character, He's going to have a pretty huge influence on how you live.

So . . . Is He?

To be honest, a lot of my dreams are about me. My goals center around my own personal success, security for my family, and growth in my own character and health. Sure, I tie Jesus into those dreams when I think of it, but most of the time, He's not the main event. It's the same for my day-to-day decisions. Yes, I'm seeking God in prayer for guidance, but it's usually so that I don't stumble and fall, not so that He can get more glory through my life.

MOST HIGH

This is a beautiful invitation! What if our worship didn't have to stop when we walked out of the church building? We've spent this whole study learning the miraculous wonders of our King. He's a God who hears us, a God who knows us intimately, a God who's jealous for us, a God who sees us, a God who won our salvation, a God of friendship, and a God who is mind-bendingly holy. That's just the tip of the iceberg of the praiseworthy things about our Father! One day a week is not enough to contain all the praise and worship He's worth! So the only natural thing to do is to let that worship flow into every single breath and step we take.

+ Find Romans 12:1 and copy it down in the space below.

What would true and sacrificial life-worship look like for you?

Maybe you worship through the music you choose to listen to on your drive to work. You worship through the way you speak about your friends (and your enemies). You worship through the way you serve your community. You worship through what you watch, through the way you handle conflict, and through the way you structure your schedule.

Even your inner life can be worship. What if you could view your little decisions as acts of worship? What if your dreams could be worship, like David's? What if your thoughts could be a constant reel of praise to God?

Sounds impossible, right? But, as we'll see as we continue reading, God can do whatever He wants in you, through you, and for you.

THINK IT THROUGH!

+ What are your favorite ways to worship God?

+ What part of your day-to-day life currently isn't bringing glory and praise to God? What would it look like for that area to turn to worship?

MOST HIGH

Now, what we're about to read is perhaps one of the most important passages in the Old Testament. Get your highlighter ready!

Read 2 Samuel 7:4-17.

+ What stands out to you about this passage?

Sheesh! This always happens. Right when I think I'm impressed by a person in the Bible, God comes in and blows everything out of the water. He is so *good!* He is so *kind!* And He is so *unexpected.*

3. God doesn't need you, but He wants you.

Let's grab some context real quick. Nathan, who we can think of as Samuel's replacement as prophet, had originally OK'd David's plan to build a temple. I mean, it sounded like a good thing to do, right? But God redirected Him later that night.

Essentially, God's message for King David was, *I don't need you to build me a house. In fact, I'll do you one better. I'm going to build my own house through you.*

08 / GOD, WORTHY OF WORSHIP

I've got goose bumps just thinking about it! And as the message from God goes on, it just keeps getting better and better.

Fill in the blanks from 2 Samuel 7:11b-13.

*"'The L*ORD *declares to you that the L*ORD *himself will establish a _____ for you: When your days are over and you rest with your ancestors, I will raise up your offspring to succeed you, your own flesh and blood, and I will establish his _____. He is the one who will build a house for my Name, and I will establish the throne of his kingdom _____."'*

I think directly, this prophecy is about Solomon, David's son who actually ended up being the one to build the temple in Jerusalem (1 Chronicles 22:6). His own flesh and blood, the next king who God grew the kingdom of Israel through.

But . . . Did you catch that last word? *Forever.*

There's only one Kingdom that has the power to last forever. And it's the Kingdom God established through His son, Jesus.

This is why this passage of Scripture is so crucial to the narrative of the whole Bible! Jesus, a descendant of King David, established a new, forever temple through His death and resurrection. Jesus secured a permanent inheritance for His people. Jesus gave them a home in Heaven that could not be disturbed. Only Jesus's Kingdom can endure forever.

MOST HIGH

> *"Jesus went into Galilee, proclaiming the good news of God. 'The time has come,' he said. 'The kingdom of God has come near. Repent and believe the good news!'"*
> Mark 1:14b-15 (emphasis added)

So what does this all mean for us as we seek to live a life sold-out and undignified for God? What does it mean that God chose to establish His home through us instead of waiting for us to build it for Him? *It means that He doesn't need our worship, but He wants our hearts.*

I think we can fall into the trap of viewing our worship like it's something God needs. We subconsciously assume that God relies on our worship to bolster His power. We assume the louder we sing or the better we act, the stronger His presence will move.

But that's just not how God works.

Yes, it's beautiful that we worship God. Yes, it's crucial that we put our faith and belief in His Son and His salvation. Yes, He loves that we want to build Him temples through our lives sold-out for Him. *But He doesn't need us!*

This seems so upside down, but it has the power to change everything for us! Our God doesn't rely on us for anything, we can't offer Him anything He doesn't already have, and He has no needs we can fulfill. *Yet still He wants us!* This is the miracle of the God worth our worship! He loves us so much that He wants to build His Kingdom through us! He cares about us so much that He delights in our presence! He wants our hearts so much that our praises are like incense rising up to Heaven, a pleasing aroma!

The pressure to perform is off! Suddenly, we can worship undignified and too-much because we know it's just icing on God's cake, not a prerequisite for love. Somehow, we are empowered to look to God in every little

08 / GOD, WORTHY OF WORSHIP

moment—not because His plans are riding solely on our shoulders but because we are secure in the knowledge that He looks at us with love and delight!

Sister, He doesn't need you! Yet still He wants you!

Once we realize how firmly planted we are in God's ability to rule the world on His own, the more free we are to worship Him. And, honestly, when we really let His majesty sink in, the more *empowered* we are to go all-out for Him! This is for the girl who feels like worship is an obligation, for the girl who wonders if her all-out praise is even noticed, and for the girl who has never stepped into worship as a way of life.

You are so loved. And out of that love, you get to praise the Lover. I want to be "too much" for Jesus until my very last breath here on this earth. Are you with me?

NOTES:

CONVERSATION

1. Think about it . . . How might you respond if Jesus showed up in the room?

2. Have you ever felt shame about the way you worshiped the Lord or been tempted to shame someone else for their worship? Why do you think that is?

STARTERS

3. Do you ever feel tempted to earn God's love? Why or why not? (Bonus: Look up some Scripture verses to read over yourself when those thoughts come in!)

4. We love that God invites us to create opportunities for worship in our day-to-day lives! Brainstorm two or three ways you can step into life-worship this week.

GOD WHO FORGIVES

MOST HIGH

God Who Forgives

> *Buckle up because we've got a tough one this week! To really look at the wonder of God's forgiveness, we have to examine the sins that lead us to need that forgiveness in the first place. Join us as we read Bathsheba and David's story of pain and redemption and allow it to turn our eyes toward God.*

2 Samuel 11:1 – 12:15

You've been holding your breath. For days. For weeks. For *years*.

You walk with a limp from the brick in your backpack you've never told anyone about.

A giant sits on your chest, but you still manage to smile, shake hands, and get good grades.

A part of you—and only you know how big that part is—is wasting away, day by day.

> "When I kept silent, my bones wasted away through my groaning all day long. For day and night your hand was heavy on me; my strength was sapped as in the heat of summer."
> Psalm 32:3–4

09 / GOD WHO FORGIVES

This week's conversation is going to be heavy. It's unavoidable when our source material is tragic and heartbreaking. But, in the upside-down way He normally operates, I believe God has a new lightness for us to experience through the heaviness. Do you need the weight of unconfessed sin off your shoulders? Then this chapter is for you.

Read 2 Samuel 11.

+ In your own words, summarize what happened in chapter 11.

We've jumped forward a few chapters from where we left off last week as God renewed His covenant with David and his descendants, hinting at the Savior to come. Between then and now, David's been on a roll, winning battles left and right. You could say he's hit his "peak" as king of Israel. But a steep climb to a high summit usually means a fast fall is ahead. And 2 Samuel chapter 11 records David's tragic downward stumble.

1. We sin (and sin, and sin, and sin).

MOST HIGH

It's a classic story, one you've likely heard before in your time around the Christian church or even in popular culture. David catches sight of a beautiful woman bathing on the roof of her home, and he summons her to the castle to sleep with him. Bathsheba—wife of Uriah the Hittite—becomes pregnant from the illicit union, prompting David to attempt some damage control. He tries to get Uriah to sleep with Bathsheba, hoping to pass the child off as his, but no luck. So David steps even deeper into the hole he's digging for himself and arranges for Uriah to be murdered. With that roadblock out of the way, David is free to steal Bathsheba from her home and marry her in the midst of her grief of an unexpected pregnancy and a dead husband.

It reminds me of what happened in the Garden of Eden—the very first sin. David saw something that looked pleasing to him (like Eve saw the forbidden fruit), he took what he wasn't allowed to have, and he sinned. And, as a result, his life would never be the same, just as it was all those years ago for the very first humans in Genesis 3.[1] And what really hurts as we read the story is the way it keeps getting worse and worse. We read it clutching onto our seats, dreading each decision David makes that takes him further into his own destruction.

David sinned. Then he sinned, and sinned, and sinned some more.

We could empathize with Bathsheba, the girl who was abruptly dragged into a life she never chose for herself, a life of tragedy, heartbreak, and confusion. We could empathize with Uriah, the innocent man who was wronged and died with his honor still intact, suffering for the sins of others. In so many moments in our lives, we are Bathsheba and we are Uriah.

But think of that breath you've been holding in. Think of that brick you carry around. Think of that weight on your chest. That one was all you. In your unconfessed sin, you're David in this story.

09 / GOD WHO FORGIVES

It's a fact of life. We sin. Then we sin, and sin, and sin some more.

I struggled when planning this chapter because this whole book is supposed to be about *God*, right? How can we spend a whole chapter floating in David's meltdown and relating it to our own struggles? Aren't we supposed to be looking at the Lord for His character?

But that's just the thing! There is nothing that brings us to the feet of the Lord more than the reality of just how much we need Him. It's those bricks we carry around—the sin that wants nothing more than to separate us from our King—that force us to make eye contact with God. We take our failures and sins out one by one and offer them to the only One who's able to do something about them.

The miracle of God's forgiveness only feels like a miracle when you realize you're desperate for it.

I'll be the first to admit that I'm David more often than I'm not. I mean, if you've made it this far into the study then you know I'm a hot mess. I sin, and sin, and sin, and sin. Bricks pile up on my shoulders faster than I can name them and heavier than I know how to deal with—the weight of lust, selfishness, and anger taking my breath away.

What are yours? Maybe your brick is that sneaky link you haven't told your friends about. Maybe yours is the drinking habit you keep hidden under your dorm bed. Maybe yours is masturbation, smoking, speeding, or pride.

I can guarantee that there's something in your life that makes you David. It's the sin that puts a shovel in your hand and forces you to dig and dig and dig because the alternative (admitting to your sin and changing your ways) feels impossible, improbable, and honestly unappealing. And if you're the girl who feels like she doesn't have one, I wonder if there's

MOST HIGH

something hidden and lurking under the surface, that God might want to reveal this week.

But are your bones hurting like mine are? We can't keep going like this. Something's got to change.

+ Get super vulnerable here. What's your "brick," the unconfessed sin that's been weighing you down?

I think David would have been content to keep going down his path of destruction were it not for God's intervention. And, really, who are we to judge?

Read 2 Samuel 12:1-13.

Nathan, the prophet we met last week, showed up to set David straight approximately one year after his initial sin with Bathsheba. (Let that sink in . . . David had been living with the brick of unconfessed sin weighing him down for a whole *year*.) But notice the little detail we might overlook in verse 1.

+ Who sent Nathan to confront David about his sin?

09 / GOD WHO FORGIVES

David might have been cool with staying in his sin, but God certainly wasn't. And that brings us right to our second point:

2. God leads us to repentance.

Through God's direction, Nathan told David a hypothetical story about a man and a lamb. After hearing about a man who stole his neighbors only lamb, David was furious, demanding retribution. Now, for us as readers, the comparisons between the lamb's story and the story of David's sin are pretty clear, but David needed a little prompting. Nathan had to give it to him straight.

> *"'You are the man!'"*
> *2 Samuel 12:7 (excerpt)*

The mission was clear: David was the man in the story who stole his neighbor's only lamb, and he needed to repent ASAP. And to do that, he needed to acknowledge his sin instead of continuing to hide it, avoid it, and justify it.

+ Do you ever try to hide, avoid, or justify your sin? How does this show up in your life?

Repentance, meaning an acknowledgement of sin that includes confession and action, is pretty out of vogue these days in our modern culture. Even in Christian circles where it should be a hot topic (Jesus talked about it a *lot!*

MOST HIGH

Check out Matthew 4:17 for example.), we avoid it in favor of sweeter, easier conversations. We love to talk about God's kindness, patience, and grace, and we're content to overlook the consequences and aftereffects of our sin.

But just because we're comfortable ignoring repentance doesn't mean that God is. In fact, His very character is meant to lead us closer to it!

Fill in the blanks from Romans 2:4.

"Or do you show contempt for the riches of his kindness, forbearance and patience, not realizing that God's _____ is intended to lead you to _____?"

But if God's kindness leads us toward repentance, why don't we repent more often? Why is it the last thing on our minds? Why does it almost never come up in Bible studies or Sunday services?

Because acknowledging sin is hard!

Think about why David must have spent so long running away from the consequences of his actions. They must have weighed so heavily on him! He was a *king*, literally charged with upholding justice, and he had unlawfully killed someone. He had just danced before the Lord in worship a few chapters before, and then he slept with another guy's wife. His shame was always present as he was faced daily with a pregnant and grieving Bathsheba.

Consider your own sin. Do you love to talk about your lying problem? Do you happily share the news of your secret porn addiction in every job interview? Do you sit and ponder the consequences of that gossip sesh in your morning quiet time? Our human nature wants us to conceal, to hide, and to push down everything that doesn't match up to God's ideal. We're embarrassed, we're ashamed, and honestly, sometimes we don't really want to change.

09 / GOD WHO FORGIVES

+ **Why do you think you've been holding on to your unconfessed sin? What's been holding you back from repentance?**

But that's where the kindness of God comes in. There's this story in the New Testament that you've probably read about Jesus and a woman at a well (check out John 4 if you need a refresher). Through their conversation, Jesus reveals that He knows about her past issues with lust and adultery. Now, if that were me and some random dude started rattling off all my sins, I would have been running for the hills. But that's not how this woman responds.

> *"Many of the Samaritans from that town believed in him because of the woman's testimony, 'He told me everything I ever did.'"*
> *John 4:39 (emphasis added)*

The woman's testimony—what she shouted in the streets for all to hear—was that Jesus had laid her sins bare before her. That doesn't sound like a woman filled with shame! Jesus is so kind, so full of mercy, and so approachable that shame isn't an option when we bring our mistakes and missteps before Him and lay them at His feet.

When you know the character of the One you're confessing to, telling Him everything becomes as easy as breathing—even the ugliest parts of you. And it seems like David was met with the character of God, too. Check out his response after Nathan delivered God's message.

MOST HIGH

"'I have sinned against the Lord.'"
2 Samuel 12:13a

It was simple—no magic words or perfect prayers. David simply met his sin head-on and placed it in the hands of God. And what happened next was a *miracle*.

3. God forgives.

"Then David said to Nathan, 'I have sinned against the Lord.' Nathan replied, 'The Lord has taken away your sin. You are not going to die. But because by doing this you have shown utter contempt for the Lord, the son born to you will die.'"
2 Samuel 12:13–14

+ Look at the verse above and circle the miracle. (Hint: it's the first sentence of Nathan's reply.)

The Lord has taken away your sin . . .

Gosh, imagine what that would feel like. Imagine if the weight you've been carrying for so long could be taken away. That's the power of God's forgiveness, something beautiful and mystifying that David became well-acquainted with.

09 / GOD WHO FORGIVES

Let's look back at Psalm 32, the psalm David wrote about this very moment in his life.

> Read Psalm 32.

+ Which verses stick out to you from this Psalm?

Verses 3 and 4 feel familiar. We know what the wasting away of silence feels like; we know the groaning caused by the weight of unconfessed sin. We are well-acquainted with the sapping of strength and the heavy hand of conviction.

But things start to change in verse 5.

I've got goose bumps just thinking about it! And as the message from God goes on, it just keeps getting better and better.

> *"Then I acknowledged my sin to you and did not cover up my iniquity. I said, 'I will confess my transgressions to the Lord.' And you forgave the guilt of my sin."*
> *Psalm 32:5*

MOST HIGH

David, with his repentant and broken heart on display after holding back for so long, laid his sin bare and brought it right to the Lord. *And God forgave him.*

To David, forgiveness felt like safety (verse 6). It felt like being held and protected by the Lord, hidden in Him instead of hidden from Him (verse 7). It felt like guidance for a new, unburdened future covered in His love (verse 8). God's forgiveness reminded David that He was no longer surrounded by the sin ever before him, but instead he was surrounded by unfailing and unfaltering love (verse 10).

What would it feel like for you?

The Bible says that "as far as the east is from the west, so far has he removed our transgressions from us" (Psalm 103:12). What if God, through a moment of repentance, could take your brick and throw it away, so far that you couldn't possibly reach it again? So far away that He forgets about it, so far away that *you* forget about it?

It sounds impossible, but if we've learned anything about God in this study, it's that impossible never stops Him. Do you want to feel a new lightness? Do you want that film reel of every time you made a mistake to stop playing in your head? Do you want a new kind of security in your faith you couldn't have imagined? That's what the forgiveness of God offers! He loves to give it; we've just gotta be willing to receive it.

09 / GOD WHO FORGIVES

Fill in the blanks from 1 John 1:9.

"If we _____ our sins, he is faithful and just and will _____ us our sins and _____ us from all unrighteousness."

The kindness of God and the weight of your sin leads you to confession and repentance. And God is so good and so faithful to forgive because He loves you that much!

But I know what you're thinking . . . *What about the consequences of David's actions?* We read in 2 Samuel 13 that there were actually a lot of ramifications, including the loss of the innocent child conceived in David's sin. What do we do with that?

+ Look back at 1 John 1:9 above and underline "cleanse us from all unrighteousness."

God's forgiveness isn't just a feeling; it's an action. We can't just tell God we're sorry about our sin then go back to vaping in the school library, sleeping around, or stealing from Target. No way! He is in the business of cleansing our unrighteousness, healing us and teaching us so we never take on the weight of those sins again.

David had to face the consequences of his actions, many of which were dire. We have to do the same. God says that we need to *kill* our sinful nature (Romans 8:31), and I've gotta say . . . killing hurts! Of course the cleansing of our souls can feel like heart surgery! God is way too good to leave your forgiveness halfway done.

THINK IT THROUGH!

+ **What do you think it would feel like to receive God's forgiveness in your area of sin? (Look back at Psalm 32 if you need inspiration!)**

+ **Consider: What might be the harder parts of the "cleansing" of your spirit (e.g., ending a relationship, having a hard conversation, asking for help and accountability, etc.)? Which consequences might you have to face (e.g., losing that position, hurting your reputation, facing discipline, etc.)?**

09 / GOD WHO FORGIVES

Let's wrap this up. We sin, God leads us to repentance, and God, in His kindness, offers us His miraculous forgiveness. So where does that leave us? What's next?

> *"Then David comforted his wife Bathsheba, and he went to her and made love to her. She gave birth to a son, and they named him Solomon. The LORD loved him;"*
> 2 Samuel 12:24

In the midst of tragedy and loss, God gave the sweetest gift to David and Bathsheba: a baby named Solomon. And that baby would grow to become the next great king of Israel, the one who would build the temple David dreamed of and would be renowned for his wisdom. And that little baby Solomon would be the great-great-great (and many more greats) grandfather of Jesus Christ.

Through a sin-studded mess, God chose to birth His Son, Savior of the world.

That, right there, is hope for you and me. No matter how stuck you feel in your sin and your struggles, you are never too far gone. God loves to forgive, and He has a grand redemption story planned for your life. Today, allow Him to take that burden off your back. He has a better future in store for you, right within your grasp.

NOTES:

CONVERSATION

1. Alright, let's get real . . . What's your "brick"? How long has this sin been weighing on your heart? What's been getting in the way of confession and repentance in this area?

2. The Lord used Nathan to call out David's secret sin. Who in your life would do this for you? If you shared your "brick" with this person, what would it look like? Would they point you to the Lord's forgiveness, or would they allow you to keep it a secret?

STARTERS

3. It's in God's nature to be kind and to forgive. What do you think has been holding you back from receiving that kindness and forgiveness?

4. Look back at Psalm 32. Which verse do you want to hold onto this week?

Bonus! We encourage you to take some time to pray together as a group over what we talked about this week. God has freedom in store for you!

GOD WHO DELIGHTS

MOST HIGH

God Who Delights

> *How in the world are we already done with our study of 1 and 2 Samuel? God has moved in miraculous ways this semester as He's revealed His heart to us through His Word. Let's praise Him for what He's done and trust Him for what He will do in the future!*

2 Samuel 22

It feels like we've squeezed the scroll of Samuel for everything it's worth, searching every nook and cranny for glimpses of God. But at the same time, it also feels like we've barely scratched the surface. There are a million stones we have yet to turn over, a million more ways to find God in these two Old Testament books.

But, ready or not, we've reached the end of our journey together. This is it. *Chapter 10 of Most High.*

There were a lot of different directions we could have taken this final installment. In between where we left off last week in 2 Samuel 12 and the end of the book, there's rebellion, fratricide, lots of murder, political intrigue, and even a guy who dies because his hair got stuck in a tree. (Yup, that actually happened!) And don't get me wrong, all of these stories are important! You can find the heart and character of God in all of them if you look hard enough, and I encourage you to dive into them in your own time.

10 / GOD WHO DELIGHTS

Unfortunately, we only have time in our study together for one more piece of Scripture. So we're jumping to 2 Samuel chapter 22, a beautiful song that seems to randomly appear in the midst of tragedy.

Read 2 Samuel 22.

+ Find three verses that stand out to you about the character of God from this chapter and copy them in the spaces below.

This song (or psalm) written by David could hold its own against any classic love song or Shakespearean sonnet. It's tender and intimate and majestic and *pretty*. It details the ways God worked in David's life, effectively summing up the entire timeline of the events we've spent ten weeks studying. And does it remind you of anything else we've read lately?

MOST HIGH

+ Flip to 1 Samuel 2. Whose prayer is similar to David's?

Hannah and David's psalms serve as bookends for the narrative of 1 and 2 Samuel. At the beginning and at the end, the reader is reminded of a humbling fact: *God is the main character of this story.*

+ Look back at 2 Samuel 22 in your Bible and underline every time David mentions God in his song. (Hint: it's a lot!)

It's seriously crazy how we can find pretty much everything we've studied this semester contained within these fifty-one verses. In every word, we see a God who hears us, an intimate God, a jealous God, a God who sees us, a God of victory, a God of friendship, a holy God, a God worth our worship, and a God who forgives.

Now, let's add one more to that list: a God who delights in us.

> *"He brought me out into a spacious place; he rescued me because he delighted in me."*
> *2 Samuel 22:20*

We're going to spend our last adventure together breaking down this one simple verse and asking God to reveal His heart to us through it. It's a breath of fresh air after an action-packed journey through a hard-to-understand book of the Bible. Are you ready? Let's do this!

10 / GOD WHO DELIGHTS

1. *God brings us to spacious places.*

I'm claustrophobic. Tube slides on the playground? They're a no-go for me. I can't even begin to describe the panic that floods my body when I feel trapped. I'm sweating just thinking about it! But I think I'm also a little bit *life*-claustrophobic.

Let me explain what I mean. I have the tendency to view my future, what's coming ahead of me, as a shrinking box. I anticipate tight spaces closing in on me, every decision I make leading me further to a trapdoor. I subconsciously assume that what I have now is the best it's going to get, living by the mantra that "things can always get worse."

Oof. Do you find yourself living with this mindset, too? You finish up a semester of school—hard-won grades and a long-anticipated summer— but you're already gearing up for next semester to be even harder. You start talking to a new guy, but you're already dreading how it's going to end— probably like how your last relationship ended, right? You have a good day, finally, but it goes downhill quickly because you know the feeling can't last.

Yes, we are promised trouble in this world (John 16:33), but somehow, we serve a God who can and will lead us to *spacious places*. We serve a God who calls us to believe that He has better ahead, that He has more in store for us, and that He is capable of widening our little boxes in astronomical and miraculous ways.

MOST HIGH

Fill in the blanks from Jeremiah 29:11.

"'For I know the plans I have for you,' declares the LORD, 'plans to _____ you and not to harm you, plans to give you ____ and a _____.'"

This verse comes from a word of the Lord that was delivered to a prophet named Jeremiah in the midst of the Baylonian exile, one of the lowest low points in the Israelites' history. They'd been captured, their city destroyed (yes, the very city David established in 2 Samuel!), and if anyone had the right to be life-claustrophobic—to doubt that God had "spacious places" ahead for them—it was these guys.

But in that terrible season, God encouraged them to believe that He had good plans in store for them, despite the current circumstance. Is it possible that He's asking us to believe the same? I don't know about you, but I'd much rather believe that God has a spacious season ahead over a never-ending tube slide.

+ What's the next season you're anticipating in your life? Consider: are you thinking about it in a "claustrophobic" or "spacious" way? Why do you think so?

So we know that God brings us to spacious places—something David definitely learned after God brought him from hiding in caves to living in a palace—but I think the next part of the verse may be even more groundbreaking.

10 / GOD WHO DELIGHTS

"he rescued me"
2 Samuel 22:20 (excerpt)

2. *God rescued us.*

Do you ever watch those little "verse of the day" videos that pop up on the Bible app? I've gotta admit, I probably only see them about 20 percent of the time. Sure, I have the widget set up on my phone so the verse of the day pops up first thing, but diving any deeper than that usually depends on if I accidentally open Instagram first and get distracted.

Well, today I checked it out (all glory to God, LOL). The verse of the day was one I'd heard lots of times, especially in Sunday school growing up.

> *"Taste and see that the LORD is good; blessed is the one who takes refuge in him."*
> *Psalm 34:8*

The video was from a man named Edgar. He asked me to close my eyes and remember a taste that stands out from my childhood. For him, it was choco-bananas he ate on his grandpa's front porch in Guatemala City. I immediately pictured the taste of Cocoa Pebbles, my breakfast of choice for most of my younger years.

Remembering the taste immediately brought me back to early mornings before school, barely awake and pouring milk into a blue bowl. The taste made the memory stronger, reminding me what it felt like and bringing me back to a different time.

MOST HIGH

Maybe that's what David meant when He said to *taste* the Lord's goodness in Psalm 34. (Yes, of course it's a David psalm! God's cool like that.) A vague memory of God's goodness or a bland assumption of His character can't compare to a visceral taste of His presence and sweetness in your life. When life gets rough and God begins to feel distant, all we need to do is remember the taste of His goodness, and we're immediately reminded of His presence and brought into gratitude.

So, if God rescued you, it's crucial to *remember* that rescue! And let's be real . . . If you have given your life to Jesus, you have been rescued! The gospel making its way into your heart and life and transforming you is the sweetest-tasting rescue there is. But there are lots of other "little" rescues God gives us along the way as we walk with Him.

You've probably been encouraged a million times to choose gratitude and to be thankful and to stand firm on the ways God's been good to you in the past—but I'm going to tell you again. The second we forget the "taste" of God's rescue, that's the very second we become in danger of not trusting God for His rescue in the future. That's the very moment when we can be tempted to doubt His character.

When I remember the time God miraculously healed me from a years-long battle with chronic illness, I can believe that He will be a healer in this season, too.

When I remember the time God comforted me in the depths of depression, I can believe that He is a comforter even here and now.

When I remember the taste of God's power I experienced when I first gave my life to Him, I can believe that He has a fresh wave of power for my life, even all these years later.

Sister, it's a simple reminder but a necessary one, for this season and the seasons to come: remember what God's rescue tastes like.

10 / GOD WHO DELIGHTS

+ **What "taste" of God's rescue, goodness, or presence can you remember? Maybe it's a moment from your childhood, a feeling of His presence in a particularly powerful worship night, a time He came through for you, or even the moment you gave your life to Jesus for the first time. Write about the memory below.**

[ ]

Alright, one last puzzle piece. And I've gotta say . . . This might be my favorite one.

3. God delights in us!

I had coffee with a freshman girl a few weeks ago, and she was going through a hard time in her life. She was scared and alone in a new city, homesick, and watching as things in her personal life crumbled one by one. As she described these hard circumstances to me, she kept interjecting little Christian-isms we all know well.

Oh, but I know God is refining me through this!
God is so good to discipline His children!
I'm sure God is waiting for me on the other side of this with open arms!

MOST HIGH

In part, she was right. I mean, this girl could quote the Bible like the back of her hand. She had all the right verses memorized and all the right Hobby Lobby sayings ready. But in the midst of her mess, this sweet girl was missing the heart of her Heavenly Father.

What if God intends to take care of you in this hard season?
What if this pain isn't punishment?
What if He's walking with you through the valley, not just waiting for you to get through on your own?

I watched it click in her eyes. She had forgotten about how much the Lord *loved* her. And through the lens of that miraculous, tender love—His *delight* in her—the circumstances began to look a little different.

Look back at this week's verse!

+ Copy down 2 Samuel 22:20 below.

10 / GOD WHO DELIGHTS

Your God brings you out to spacious places. He rescues you. Why? Because He delights in you!

The Hebrew word here for "delight" is *hapes*. It means to take pleasure in or to desire. How crazy is it that God—this Most High, amazing, wonderful, other-worldly God we've spent this whole semester learning about—likes us! It brings Him pleasure to be with us! He desires our company, our attention, and our love!

> *"If I speak in the tongues of men or of angels, but do not have <u>love</u>, I am only a resounding gong or a clanging cymbal. If I have the gift of prophecy and can fathom all mysteries and all knowledge, and if I have a faith that can move mountains, but do not have <u>love</u>, I am nothing. If I give all I possess to the poor and give over my body to hardship that I may boast, but do not have <u>love</u>, I gain nothing."*
> 1 Corinthians 13:1-3 (emphasis added)

Love is the starting point and the ending. Without it, we could never hope to understand our Father and King.

Yes, our God is Most High. He thunders from Heaven, smoke coming from His nostrils and consuming fire from His mouth (2 Samuel 22:9). But, that God Most High bends low so that He can wait by your bed for you to wake up in the morning just so you can spend the day together. God doesn't just endure you, He enjoys you.

Somehow, in the midst of all His grandeur, God likes you and me. He delights in us! And that fact should change our lives.

THINK IT THROUGH!

+ **What delights you about God? Name a few of your favorite attributes of His character below.**

+ **What do you think delights the Lord about you? Jot down His favorite of your characteristics.**

10 / GOD WHO DELIGHTS

My hope for you as we round out this study is that you can't help but look at God with fresh eyes, a new perspective, and a tender heart. I'm imagining Delight girls across the nation making eye contact with their Creator and handing Him their hearts, trusting that He can take care of them. I'm imagining so many women dropping the weight of being the center of their own lives and turning to Jesus, the real and true main character—the One who was and is and is to come (Revelation 1:8).

What better way to end this than with praise!? Let's write our own songs of praise to God for what He's done for us these past ten weeks, ten years, or ten lifetimes. Just as David did all those years ago, write your own "song of praise" to a worthy, Most High King.

+ Fill this box with praise and gratitude! It doesn't have to be pretty, eloquent, or poetic. Just delight in Him!

_____ *(your name) sang to the Lord the words of this song when the Lord delivered* _____ *(your name) from the hand of all her enemies...*

CONVERSATION

1. Where would you rate yourself on the scale below when it comes to how you view your future? Why did you answer that way?

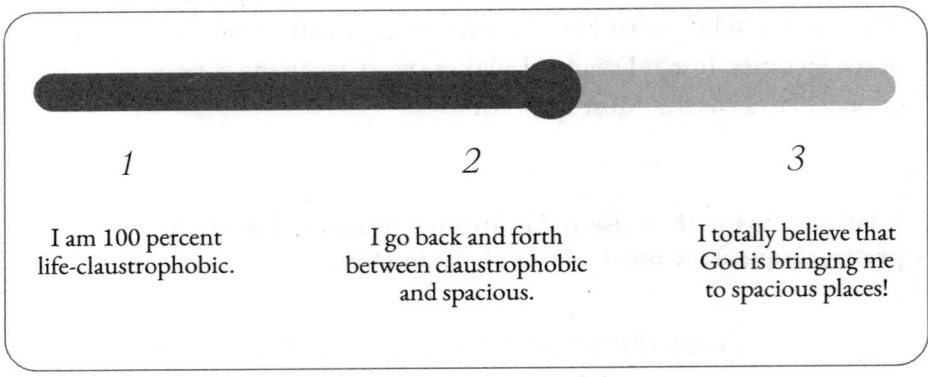

1	2	3
I am 100 percent life-claustrophobic.	I go back and forth between claustrophobic and spacious.	I totally believe that God is bringing me to spacious places!

2. What does gratitude look like in your life these days? How might you want to grow that discipline or step deeper into it?

STARTERS

3. Be honest . . . Do you ever struggle to feel God's delight in you? Why do you think that is?

4. We just spent ten weeks studying God's character and finding His heart in 1 and 2 Samuel. What was your biggest takeaway from this study?

NOTES

Chapter 1:
1. MacArthur, John. *1 Samuel: The Lives of Samuel and Saul.* Nelson Books, 2016, p. 9.

Chapter 3:
1. MacArthur, John. *1 Samuel: The Lives of Samuel and Saul.* Nelson Books, 2016, p. 51.

Chapter 5:
1. MacArthur, John. *1 Samuel: The Lives of Samuel and Saul.* Nelson Books, 2016, p. 143.

2. See a victory (by Elevation Worship)
Elevation Worship. "See A Victory." *At Midnight - EP*, Elevation Worship Records,
2020. Spotify, https://open.spotify.com/track/0wtFB7vmIRecZhXQbDQ9Z1?si=6c50c2e1fc644bb0.

Chapter 6:
1. Goldingay, John. *1 and 2 Samuel for Everyone.* Westminster John Knox Press, 2011, p. 87.

Chapter 7:
1. Daniel Sarlo and John T. Swann, "Ark of the Covenant," ed. John D. Barry et al., *The Lexham Bible Dictionary* (Bellingham, WA: Lexham Press, 2016).

2. Sarlo, Daniel and Swann, John T. "Ark of the Covenant." The Lexham Bible Dictionary, edited by John D. Barry, et al., Lexham Press, 2016.

3. *Renovation of the heart,* dallas willard
Willard, Dallas, Renovations of the Heart. NavPress, 2002

Chapter 9:
1. MacArthur, John. *2 Samuel: David's Heart Revealed.* Nelson Books, 2016, p. 52.

About the Author!

Hey! I'm Maggie!

I am working my *dream job* as Curriculum Development Coordinator here at Delight Ministries. I like to think of myself as Delight's translator. My job is to take God's powerful, perfect, and active Word and present it to college women in a way that helps them see how relevant it is for their own lives . . . *AND I LOVE IT!*

On the weekends, catch me serving in my church's kids ministry with my husband and writing for Delight Worship. I love to read, I'm a die-hard Swiftie, and I'll never say no to a *Twilight* marathon.

CONTRIBUTORS

Editing Team:
Theological Editing by Aubrey Meredith
Editing by Maddie Grimes

Design:
Faith Hyman

Special Thanks To:
Abby Elias
Leesa Fletcher
Brecken Mills
Christina Pierre
Emily Mikus
Emily Stevens
Emma Lehman
Gracie Woods
Haley Moser
Jojo Beaumariage
Riley Allen
Sarah Sohre

DELIGHT WORSHIP

It all started with a question . . . *What if we could write worship music for college women?*

SO WE DID! Delight Worship is intentional music created to connect college women to the heart of Jesus.

Listen today!

START A DELIGHT

Help us spread the word about Delight!

There are thousands of college women all across the country that need Christ-centered community but have no idea Delight exists!!! We need women like you to help spread the word.

If this community has impacted your life in any way, don't you want to help other women experience it, too?

If you know a friend who loves Jesus and who would make an amazing Delight leader—tell her about Delight! With just a few texts you could indirectly reach hundreds of college women on another campus!

How cool is that?!

www.delightministries.com

Point them to our website where they can sign up to bring Delight to their campus! Once they sign up, they will hear from us and will get everything they need to make this community happen at their university.

So . . . send a couple texts, call a couple friends, maybe post about it on your socials, and let's reach a million more college women together!

YEARBOOK PAGE

Fill these pages with sweet notes from your Delight community!

For more information, resources,
or encouragement head to . . .

www.delightministries.com